Praise for *Argument-Based Validation in Testing and Assessment*

"Chapelle's *Argument-Based Validation in Testing and Assessment* is among the best-written texts on test validity. It is an up-to-date, cogent presentation from a logical—as opposed to strictly psychometric—perspective."

— Shlomo Sawilowsky, Wayne State University

"This text addresses complex philosophical discussions related to validity and reliability in an accessible way. It models a way of thinking about assessment decisions that many of our students need to be successful in their future work!"

— Amanda C. La Guardia, University of Cincinnati

ARGUMENT-BASED VALIDATION IN TESTING AND ASSESSMENT

Quantitative Applications in the Social Sciences

A SAGE PUBLICATIONS SERIES

Quantitative Applications in the Social Sciences

A SAGE PUBLICATIONS SERIES

For Susan

Sara Miller McCune founded SAGE Publishing in 1965 to support the dissemination of usable knowledge and educate a global community. SAGE publishes more than 1000 journals and over 800 new books each year, spanning a wide range of subject areas. Our growing selection of library products includes archives, data, case studies and video. SAGE remains majority owned by our founder and after her lifetime will become owned by a charitable trust that secures the company's continued independence.

Los Angeles | London | New Delhi | Singapore | Washington DC | Melbourne

ARGUMENT-BASED VALIDATION IN TESTING AND ASSESSMENT

Carol A. Chapelle

Iowa State University

Los Angeles | London | New Delhi
Singapore | Washington DC | Melbourne

FOR INFORMATION:

SAGE Publications, Inc.
2455 Teller Road
Thousand Oaks, California 91320
E-mail: order@sagepub.com

SAGE Publications Ltd.
1 Oliver's Yard
55 City Road
London, EC1Y 1SP
United Kingdom

SAGE Publications India Pvt. Ltd.
B 1/I 1 Mohan Cooperative Industrial Area
Mathura Road, New Delhi 110 044
India

SAGE Publications Asia-Pacific Pte. Ltd.
18 Cross Street #10-10/11/12
China Square Central
Singapore 048423

Printed in the United States of America

LCCN 2019047108

ISBN 978-1-5443-3448-6

SUSTAINABLE FORESTRY INITIATIVE

Certified Sourcing
www.sfiprogram.org
SFI-00756

This book is printed on acid-free paper.

Acquisitions Editor: Helen Salmon
Editorial Assistant: Megan O'Heffernan
Production Editor: Rebecca Lee
Copy Editor: Diana Breti
Typesetter: Hurix Digital
Proofreader: Wendy Jo Dymond
Indexer: Beth Nauman-Montana
Cover Designer: Candice Harman
Marketing Manager: Shari Countryman

20 21 22 23 24 10 9 8 7 6 5 4 3 2 1

CONTENTS

LIST OF TABLES

LIST OF FIGURES

SERIES EDITOR'S INTRODUCTION

I am pleased to introduce *Argument-Based Validation in Testing and Assessment*, by Carol A. Chapelle. This volume explains and demonstrates how to implement the validity guidelines promulgated by the *Standards for Educational and Psychological Testing*. In contrast to most QASS volumes, which present a statistical technique or set of techniques, the method presented in this volume is a framework, logic, and approach. The primary audience is students and practitioners in psychology and educational testing, but this "little green cover" will be of broad interest as well.

Partly because of the focus on the construction of arguments, but also because of clear writing and organization, the volume is broadly accessible. Professor Chapelle charts the evolution of "validation" across editions of the *Standards* in the first chapter. The second chapter provides a high-level overview of the argument-based validation framework, drawing on the work of Michael Kane. The chapters that follow address seven inferences that can compose a validity argument: domain definition (appropriate content), evaluation (insensitivity to test conditions), generalization (consistent performance), explanation (capture of the intended construct), extrapolation (extension beyond the specific items), utilization (usefulness for a purpose), and consequence implication (positive outcomes of that use). One of the contributions of the volume is to introduce vocabulary specific to the argument-based validation approach (e.g., the detail used to support inferences is organized in terms of "warrants," "assumptions," and "backing").

Use is the starting point for argument-based validation. Three examples demonstrate how the inferences in the framework support each of the three different uses. TOEFL iBT is a test of English proficiency used to make decisions about whom to admit among university applicants whose first language is not English. Judgments are based in part on an *extrapolation* of the score meaning from the conditions of the test to the academic setting. The MSCEIT is a test of emotional intelligence. The intended construct, in this instance, the ability to recognize and reason about emotions, *explains* the score, which is therefore claimed to be useful for investigating human abilities. The mathematics section of the Iowa Assessments was designed for a variety of uses, for example, to measure strengths and weaknesses of individual students, with the idea of identifying who might benefit from individual help. Research therefore supports the *utilization* inference.

Concise and clear, the volume will become a go-to reference for practitioners. It will also be of broad interest to social scientists interested in measurement issues, as it presents validation from a different perspective than is typical in standard texts. In the *Standards*, it is the interpretations and uses of a test that are validated, rather than the test itself. Importantly, use is viewed not only in terms of its immediate application but also in terms of the larger social consequences of the test. A focus on use also directs attention to the possibility that a test may not be appropriate for all populations and cultures. I will be bringing insights from this volume into my methods classes.

— Barbara Entwisle
Series Editor

PREFACE

Test developers, researchers, and anyone responsible for assessing human capacities would readily agree that validity is their central concern. Similarly, teachers, employers, students, parents, and researchers want the tests they use to be valid, and they expect professionals in educational and psychological testing to know how to evaluate a test's validity. Accordingly, a definition of validity has been developed and revised multiple times by the professional organizations concerned with educational and psychological testing in the United States: the American Educational Research Association (AERA), the American Psychological Association (APA), and the National Council on Measurement in Education (NCME). The guidelines produced by representatives from these organizations, *Standards for Educational and Psychological Testing* (AERA, APA, & NCME, 2014), contain a definition of validity and, as its title suggests, standards for validation of tests and assessments. The consensus definition of validity is a good starting point for this methodology book, which shows how the argument-based validation framework provides the conceptual tools required for putting into practice the guidance in the *Standards*.

The definition of validity in the current *Standards* emanates from more than 60 years of consensus building within and across the relevant professional organizations (Plake & Wise, 2014). Longtime researcher in educational measurement Shepard (2016) explained the significance of the professional consensus in this area of social science research that plays such an important role in society:

> The consensus process does not mean that this definition is absolutely right, nor is it fixed for all time. It does mean that this is the professionally defensible definition to be shared with non-experts, and it is the definition that experts and testing companies should acknowledge, if they decide to depart from it. Rather than portraying the field as hopelessly in disarray because some experts disagree, I would argue that the consensus definition provides a clear and well-organized framework for orderly debate. (p. 272)

The debate challenges the consensus definition in three primary ways. One challenge comes from professionals who question its breadth, which they see as too expansive to serve the profession (e.g., see the 1997 special issue of *Educational Measurement: Issues and Practice, 16*[2]). A second challenge questions the jurisdiction of a consensus emanating from American organizations. Zumbo (2014) pointed out that "the *Standards* is, by design, a social and cultural product that has evolved, and has been revised, by three very large educational and psychological academic professional associations based in the United States" (p. 31), but he concluded that the *Standards* has nevertheless had an influence globally. A third challenge is posed by theorists who bring questions of epistemology to bear on the definition of validity (e.g., Markus & Borsboom, 2013). Participants in the academic discussion may align themselves with one or any combination of these challenges to the definition of validity in the *Standards*.

These academic discussions of validity in testing continue in journals such as a special issue of *Assessment in Education: Principles, Policy & Practice* that featured what the introductory editorial referred to as "the great validity debate" (Newton & Baird, 2016), mirroring the opening editorial of the 1997 special issue mentioned earlier (Crocker, 1997). Newton and Baird (2016) questioned the status of the consensus view of validity presented in the *Standards* in view of continuing controversy among professionals and the variety of presentations of validity on websites of test publishers, even in the United States.

The seemingly intractable academic debate will continue, but in the meantime, test users, test developers, and testing researchers need tests, an accepted understanding of validity, and concrete methods for putting that definition into practice. Argument-based validity has figured prominently in the ongoing theoretical discussion (see, e.g., the special issue of *Journal of Educational Measurement, 50*[1]), but it was developed to address the practical need for validation practice (Kane, 2006). I am among the practitioners who have used the validity argument framework based on the concepts and tools Kane has presented over the past 25 years. Having worked on validity arguments, I can attest that fortitude is required to interpret and apply the guidance from the academic papers, which introduce new terms while assuming background knowledge of technical concepts and socially situated issues in the field. Validation is technical, complex, and value-laden work. Validation research requires language and concepts commensurate with the task.

The goal of this book, then, is not to simplify validation but instead to explain the approach that argument-based validity offers to address the task at hand. In doing so, the book provides actionable guidance for designing the overarching argument that test developers and researchers need to conceive and plan validation research. Chapter 1 provides sufficient background and context for readers to understand the concepts used in validity arguments. Chapters 2 through 6 introduce the terms used in validity argument, with concrete examples along with general principles of argument-based validity to empower readers to construct their own and critically evaluate novel validity arguments. The final chapter provides practical advice on getting started and making argument-based validity work for test developers and researchers across a variety of contexts. Overall, the book offers a path for test developers and researchers wanting to create a coherent program of validation research, by increasing their understanding of the central concern in the field.

ACKNOWLEDGMENTS

Argument-Based Validation in Testing and Assessment is the result of years of wrestling with how to conceptualize and express all that goes into validation of tests and assessments. This struggle at the nexus of theory and practice has benefited from my participation in testing projects in a variety of contexts and from the opportunity to teach and engage in validation research. I therefore express my gratitude to the students, collaborators, and scholars whose challenging questions and ideas about validation have provided me with rich learning opportunities. I am especially grateful to my colleagues in language assessment throughout the world, whose unique understanding of the issues, technical expertise, and unrelenting pursuit of better language tests have created the ideal environment for me to build a useful understanding of validation.

The book project was met with encouragement by Helen Salmon, senior acquisitions editor at SAGE and Professor Barbara Entwisle, series editor of the SAGE *Quantitative Applications in the Social Sciences* series. I am grateful to Barbara for her comments on the manuscript and for sharing her expertise in overseeing the review process with great care and attention. I thank the anonymous reviewers of both the book proposal and manuscript for their comments and suggestions, which contributed notably to the final product. In addition, I would like to acknowledge the expert editing of Diana Breti and the careful work of the production team to bring the project to successful completion. Much of the manuscript was written during the time I spent at the Institut des langues officielles et du bilinguisme/Official Languages and Bilingualism Institute at the Université d'Ottawa/University of Ottawa in Canada in 2017. I thank my colleagues, Beverly Baker and Angel Arias, at the testing division there for kindly engaging in many discussions with me about validation as the chapters of this book took shape.

SAGE and the author would like to thank the following reviewers for their feedback:

Nicole I. Caswell, East Carolina University
Tim Farnsworth, CUNY Hunter College
Sandy Gibson, The College of New Jersey
Nathan Greenauer, Pennsylvania State University, Berks
Amanda C. La Guardia, University of Cincinnati
Joni M. Lakin, Auburn University

Matthew Ryan Lavery, Bowling Green State University
Andrew Maul, University of California, Santa Barbara
Robert J. Mislevy, Educational Testing Service
Shlomo Sawilowsky, Wayne State University

ABOUT THE AUTHOR

Carol A. Chapelle is a distinguished professor in the College of Liberal Arts and Sciences at Iowa State University, where she teaches courses in second-language acquisition and assessment, including a course on argument-based validity. She has more than 30 years of experience working on research and development in testing and assessment for English as a second language, including supervision of PhD dissertation research, participation in test development projects, and advisory service for commercial, nonprofit, and government projects in testing.

Throughout her research and practice in language testing, she has explored the evolving methodological guidance for conducting validation research. She was led to the nascent concepts of argument-based validation in the early writing of Michael Kane while working on a project to summarize the validation research for the Test of English as a Foreign Language (TOEFL iBT). The team cultivated Kane's concepts into a validity argument that succeeded in providing a means for encompassing multiple types of qualitative and quantitative data within a coherent framework showing the connections across test development, test performance, and the uses of the scores. The result was a book presenting the validity argument for the TOEFL iBT, *Building a Validity Argument for the Test of English as a Foreign Language* (Chapelle, Enright, & Jamieson, 2008), which remains a rare example for researchers of a validity argument in use.

Professor Chapelle is the recipient of the 2012 Cambridge-International Language Testing Association Lifetime Achievement Award, the 2012 Educational Testing Service TOEFL Program Messick Memorial Lecture Award, and the 2015 Distinguished Scholarship and Service Award from the American Association for Applied Linguistics. She has served as co-editor of *Language Testing* (2016–2018), co-editor of the Cambridge Series in Applied Linguistics (2007–present), and founding editor of the *Encyclopedia of Applied Linguistics* (Wiley-Blackwell, 2012–present).

Chapter 1

WHAT IS ARGUMENT-BASED VALIDITY?

The title of this book includes both the terms *testing* and *assessment* because the basic concepts of argument-based validity apply to the full range of activities encompassed by testing and assessment. Tests and assessments are used to make inferences about people's capacities on the basis of a sample of their performance. In testing and assessment, the inferences are used for such purposes as placing students into classes, drawing conclusions about learning, diagnosing specific challenges, judging candidates' performance adequacy for a job, making decisions about university admissions, and certifying qualifications. Tests and assessments are widely used by educators, human resources personnel, and researchers in education, government, health professions, and business, for example. In these varying contexts, some users of tests and assessments favor one term over another, but in this book no conceptual distinction is intended as both terms are used to refer to the same process of using systematically gathered samples of performance, summarized as scores, to make inferences about human capacities from which conclusions are drawn. The professionals responsible for all facets of testing and assessment are referred to as "testers."

The central concern for testers is validity, and therefore the meaning of validity and how to conduct validation research are ongoing topics of discussion and debate in the field. As academic discussion continues, testers need to meet the many demands of society for tests that can help in making a range of decisions. Since 1954, this need has been addressed, in part, by the consensus about validity and validation research expressed in the *Standards for Educational and Psychological Testing*, referred to throughout the book as the *Standards* (American Educational Research Association [AERA], American Psychological Association [APA], and the National Council on Measurement in Education [NCME], 2014). The *Standards* was developed and is periodically revised by the American professional associations directly concerned with testing: the AERA, the APA, and the NCME (Plake & Wise, 2014). Members of these organizations include the theorists, researchers, and practitioners who formulate conceptual and methodological approaches for testing and assessment that are applied across subject areas in and beyond North America. Because of the wide use of the *Standards*, comments considered in the most recent revision came from others concerned with testing and assessment, including other professional associations (e.g., American Counseling Association and National Association of School Psychologists), testing companies (e.g., ACT and Pearson), academic and research institutions (e.g., Human Resources Research Organization), credentialing organizations (e.g., National Board of Medical Examiners), and other institutions (e.g., Fair Assess Coalition on Testing). This chapter introduces argument-based validity as a means for implementing the validity guidelines in the *Standards* and sketches the evolution of concepts about validity that have informed both the general guidance in the *Standards* and the specific conventions of argument-based validity.

Introducing Argument-Based Validity

Argument-based validity, as formulated primarily by Kane (1992, 2006, 2013), provides the conceptual tools needed to carry out the guidance in the *Standards*. The *Standards* defines validity as "the degree to which evidence and theory support the interpretations of test scores for proposed uses of test scores" (AERA et al., 2014, p. 1). This definition expressed by professionals is different from the common sense notion that validity refers to tests themselves and that tests can, therefore, be either valid or invalid. According to the *Standards*, "statements about validity should refer to particular interpretations for specified uses," and "it is incorrect to use the unqualified phrase 'the validity of the test'" (p. 1). Argument-based validity provides a means for defining the interpretations and uses of test results so that the intended interpretations and uses can be validated.

Another commonly held perception is that validation research is carried out by calculating a correlation between sets of scores on two tests. In contrast, the *Standards* alludes to a more complex process for doing validation that begins with "an explicit statement of the proposed interpretation of the test scores, along with a rationale for the relevance of the interpretation to the proposed use" (AERA et al., 2014, p. 1). In addition, propositions supporting the proposed interpretations need to be identified, and then "one can proceed with validation by obtaining empirical evidence, examining relevant literature, and/or conducting logical analyses to evaluate each of the propositions" (p. 1). Specifically, the *Standards* names five types of evidence that can be used to investigate validity: evidence based on rationales and expert judgment of test content, evidence based on the study of test takers' response processes, evidence based on statistical testing of the internal structure of response data, evidence based on relationships to other variables (including convergent and discriminate evidence), and evidence about the consequences of testing (*Standards*, pp. 13–21). These five types of evidence are intended to be integrated to make a professional judgment about validity. Overall, the *Standards* treats validation as a process of scientific hypothesis testing consisting of formulating propositions and evaluating their plausibility in view of empirical data. It also includes expert judgment and theoretical rationales in the validation process.

However, the *Standards* is not a methodology book with details about how to design a program of validation research and references to academic sources supporting its guidance. The argument-based approach to validation provides testers with a framework for conceptualizing the complex validation process suggested in the *Standards*, concepts and procedures for designing validation programs to yield the evidence called for by the *Standards*, and a common language for communicating within and across testing programs about the meaning of research results for the validity of test interpretation and use. Argument-based validation is not a single method yielding one type of validity evidence. Instead, argument-based validation encompasses a research program consisting of activities whose findings need to be integrated into a logical conclusion about the validity of test score interpretations for particular uses. Like the *Standards*, argument-based validation has its roots in an academic tradition of more than 100 years.

The Academic Tradition of Validity

The *Standards* does not make reference to the academic literature on validity, but the consensus views expressed in each successive version reflect the contemporary concepts, practices, and values of researchers in educational and psychological testing. These technical foundations have been conceived and refined over the past century (Kane, 2013; Messick, 1989; Shepard, 1993; Sireci, 2009). Playing a key role in this historical evolution have been the multiple editions of *Educational Measurement*, an authoritative edited volume published first in 1951 and then updated three times, in 1971, 1989, and 2006. Each volume contains a chapter on validity and validation research from one author's viewpoint and serves as a catalyst for discussion, research, and practice, which in turn influence the following edition of the *Standards*.

These chapters have proved to be influential because they provide useful snapshots of a dynamic evolution of concepts that remain important for testing today, and therefore build the background for argument-based validity. The four chapters in successive editions of *Educational Measurement* have been analyzed from a philosophical perspective to show how they reflect the evolution that has taken place across the social sciences (Markus & Borsboom, 2013). Such an analysis emphasizes change and disjuncture. What is needed to work with validity arguments in practice today is an understanding of the basic concepts in testing that the chapters introduce and how the roles of these concepts have shifted in validation research. Most central is the evolution in the conceptualization of what gets validated, which has shifted from the idea that the test itself is validated to the statement in the *Standards* today that interpretations and uses of a test need to be validated. This conceptual shift, which occurred in the 1950s, began to reveal the complexity of the validation process as portrayed in the chapters of the successive editions. Argument-based validity was developed as a way of managing the complexity of the process of validation, and it does so by accommodating the important concepts introduced by previous generations of testers.

1951: Validity of a Test for Its Purpose

In the first edition of *Educational Measurement*, Cureton (1951) defined validity as a characteristic of a test but acknowledged that it means "how well the test serves the purpose for which it is used" (p. 621). He defined purpose as "the function to be appraised" and "the group in which the appraisal is to be made" (p. 621). For him, validity included both the relevance of a test for its purpose and its reliability, as illustrated in Figure 1.1. Reliability was defined in terms of the size of sample of performance, whereas relevance was further defined as consisting of empirical relevance and logical relevance. The latter requires a demonstration that the test content results from an appropriate definition of the criterion domain and sampling of content from that domain. The former is demonstrated by the correlation of the test with the appropriate criterion. "A direct quantitative estimate of the test's validity is provided by the actual test-criterion correlation corrected for attenuation in the criterion scores but not for attenuation in the test scores" (p. 623). The correction for attenuation allows for treatment of the criterion measure to be interpreted as a "true" score, which refers to the proportion of the score variance that is not error. A correlation based on the true score of the criterion can be estimated from the observed score, making the procedure for calculating a validity coefficient clear. With such a straightforward procedure in place for estimating validity, Cureton had no need for construct theory, which would not have fit in the operationalist perspectives of that period.

5

Figure 1.1   Schematic Diagram of the Components of Validity as
Defined by Cureton (1951)

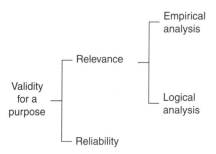

In view of the central role of the criterion measure in estimating an empirical validity coefficient, the chapter is almost singularly focused on how relevant behaviors (i.e., performance) can be identified from a "universe of behavior" (Cureton, 1951, p. 631) and assessed in a manner that will allow them to serve as criterion measures in validation studies. Ironically, criterion measures are beset by the same challenges as any test, and readers are left to conclude that a credible validity coefficient is purely hypothetical because acceptable criterion measures can be described only in hypothetical terms as a sample of performance from a defined series of criterion behaviors. In view of this irony, Cureton acknowledged the limited utility of validation research for test use:

> Often we are called upon to make action judgments on the basis of the best available tests in situations wherein we do not know what tests are the best available, nor the validities for any tests for the purposes at hand. Such situations are the rule, rather than the exception, in educational and vocational guidance, and most of the tests which are used in guidance are intelligence tests, aptitude tests, interest tests, personality tests, and the like, rather than educational achievement tests. (p. 664)

Cureton's (1951) rigorous definition of criterion scores explains some concepts that are still in use today, such as sampling of content, universe scores, and true scores. But it also created a value-laden dilemma by assembling an impossible set of requirements for researchers working within the constraints and demands of the real world. His advice was that "ideally, we should not use the term *criterion scores* for any measures that fail to meet the requirements of random or representative selection of acts from the criterion series, and unbiased observation and evaluation" (p. 632). In the real world where criterion scores never satisfy theoretical ideals and tests have consequences, Cureton cautioned, "A set of non-representative or biased criterion scores may well be less relevant to the ultimate criterion than are a set of scores on a carefully worked-out test" (p. 634). In the end, then, the acknowledged reality of educational and psychological testing falls largely outside the requirements for a validity coefficient as defined by Cureton.

1971: Validity of Test Interpretations

In the second edition of *Educational Measurement*, Cronbach's (1971) definition shifted the object of validation to the test interpretations. Underscoring the shift, he wrote, "The phrase *validation of a test* is the source of much misunderstanding. One validates, not a test, but *an interpretation of data arising from a specified procedure*" (p. 447). Cronbach saw Cureton's validity coefficient expressing prediction of a criterion measure as being too narrow, pointing out the "paradox" that it "rests on acceptance of the criterion measure as being perfectly valid (save for random error), yet common sense tells one that it is not" (p. 487).

Cronbach (1971) presented a broader conception of validation, which "examines the soundness of all the interpretations of the test—descriptive and explanatory interpretations as well as situation-bound predictions" (p. 443). He acknowledged that the 1966 edition of the *Standards* had described three types of validity—criterion-related validity, content validity, and construct validity—but for him, there were not three validities. Instead, he referred to gathering types of evidence for "*what in the end must be a comprehensive, integrated evaluation of the test*" (p. 445). As illustrated in Figure 1.2, he defined two primary types of evidence: evidence supporting the soundness of interpretations—which can be done through inquiries into content validity, educational importance, and construct validity—and evidence about the usefulness of scores for decision making about selection and placement, for example.

Cronbach (1971) framed the process of validation as scientific hypothesis testing. The hypotheses state that test takers' performance on a particular testing procedure can be interpreted as an indicator of the construct that the test is intended to measure. Drawing upon the introduction of construct validity presented by Cronbach and Meehl (1955), he saw constructs as the logical basis for interpretations and essential when score interpretations cannot be made on the basis of a criterion or a domain of content. "Whenever one classifies situations, persons, or responses, he uses constructs. The term *concepts* might be used rather than *constructs,* but the latter term emphasizes that categories are deliberate creations chosen to organize

Figure 1.2   Schematic Diagram of the Types of Investigations of Validity as Defined by Cronbach (1971)

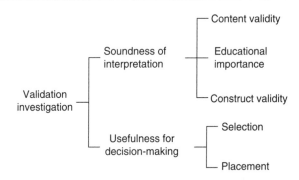

experience into general law-like statements" (Cronbach, 1971, p. 462). The lawlike statements form the basis for construct theories that are intended to explain test performance.

Test performance serves as the empirical data in the process of hypothesis testing and, therefore, must be gathered with great care through the testing procedure, which Cronbach (1971) referred to as the operational definition of the construct. An operational definition is a full description of the procedures, including test content, and the allowable variations that are repeatedly administered to gather consistent samples of test takers' performance. The consistency afforded by a good operational definition plays a critical role in gathering relevant performance data from test takers from which the tester makes inferences about the construct. Consistency, or reliability, needs to be achieved not only by gathering a sufficient number of samples of performance but also by gathering the appropriate samples of performance. Consistent performance samples play an important role in Cronbach's view of construct validation as scientific hypothesis testing because constructs ascribe meaning to systematic observations.

Cronbach's (1971) portrait of researchers engaged in scientific hypothesis testing implied scientific values of rigor and an unrelenting quest for developing theories useful for explaining test performance. The discovery-oriented values of a scientist are evident in his view of validation:

A test score has an endless list of implications, and one cannot validate the entire list. Construct validation is therefore never complete. Construct validation is better seen as an ever-extending inquiry into the processes that produce a high or low test score and into the other effects of those processes. (p. 452)

Such programs of inquiry are undertaken by a community of scientists with a common set of values motivating them to discover useful ways to define and measure constructs, which "requires the concurrence of persons who have thought deeply about the problem and have given due weight to research from laboratories with other orientations" (Cronbach, 1971, p. 480).

Cronbach's (1971) presentation of a never-ending process of construct validation in which no coefficient of construct validity exists and a series of studies does not "permit a simple summary" (p. 464) was overwhelming to many textbook writers and practitioners, and remains so today. Many textbooks today still teach students that there are three types of validity, even though by 1985 the *Standards* presented construct validity as central to a single, integrated judgment, rather than as one of three validities. Nevertheless, Cronbach's prescient vision of validation as a research program serves as the foundation for argument-based validity.

1989: Validity of Interpretations and Actions

In the third edition of *Educational Measurement*, Messick (1989) elaborated on a unitary conception of validity by defining validity as "an overall evaluative judgment of the degree to which empirical evidence and theoretical rationales support the adequacy and appropriateness of interpretations and actions based on test scores" (p. 13). Messick saw the three validities—content validity, criterion-related validity, and construct validity—as a historic idea, which promoted the poor practice of choosing one of the validities rather than engaging in the type of scientific hypothesis testing depicted by Cronbach (1971). Construct validity, for Messick, was central to all validation research, and "because content- and criterion-related evidence contribute to score meaning, they have come to be recognized as aspects of construct validity. In a sense, then, this leaves only one category, namely, construct-related evidence" (Messick, 1989, p. 20).

The distinction between types of validity and types of evidence is lost on many researchers and practitioners who continue to use the pre-1985 terminology of multiple validities and even add new types of validity (e.g., see the analysis by Newton & Shaw, 2014). However, for Messick and others viewing validation as a scientific process of investigating score meaning, the distinction between "types of validities" and "evidence for validity" is important, so much so that Messick chronicled the shift in definitions of validity from types of validity in the 1950s to the 1980s view of validity as unitary. "Types of evidence" fits well with the perspective of validation as hypothesis testing, whereas "types of validity" does not.

Constructs are central to Messick's (1989) presentation of validity. He defined a construct as a meaningful interpretation of performance consistency. Consistency, or reliability, is important because any test score, as a summary of performance, can have meaning only if the individual samples of performance mean something in combination.

The key point is that in educational and psychological measurement inferences are drawn from scores, a term used here in the most general sense of any coding or summarization of observed consistencies on a test, questionnaire, observation procedure, or other assessment device. (p. 14)

Building on Cronbach's (1971) entrée into validation as scientific hypothesis testing, Messick (1989) explored aspects of philosophy of science to lay a principled basis for defining constructs, conceptualizing validation as inquiry, and developing the facets of a unitary conception of validity. Ontologically speaking, construct meaning can be conceptualized from realist, constructivist, and realist-constructivist positions. Realists view constructs as true. A constructivist position, such as the one taken by Cronbach (1971), does not presume a search for the truth. Cronbach explicitly used the term "*usefulness*, not *truth*" (p. 477) to refer to explanatory theoretical networks of constructs. Messick (1989) presented a constructivist-realist position as a middle ground. Epistemologically speaking, Messick examined five modes of inquiry from which researchers can investigate meaning. The goal was to go beyond declaring validation to be scientific inquiry to laying out potential modes of scientific inquiry (or epistemologies) for discovery of construct meanings reflecting different ontologies. In doing so, he explicitly recognized the need to take into account the contextual social and cultural aspects of test interpretation and use.

Mesick's (1989) unitary validity is made up of four facets resulting from each of the two functions of testing (interpretation and use) being justified two ways (evidence and consequences), as shown in Figure 1.3. The evidential basis for test interpretation is construct validity. The evidential basis for test use is construct validity and relevance/utility because "*general* evidence supportive of construct validity usually needs to be buttressed by *specific* evidence of the relevance of the test to the applied purpose and the utility of the test in the applied setting" (p. 20). This means that validity inquiry encompasses the investigation of the local, cultural meanings of test scores and their use.

Figure 1.3 Schematic Diagram of the Facets of Validity as Defined by Messick (adapted from Messick, 1989, p. 20)

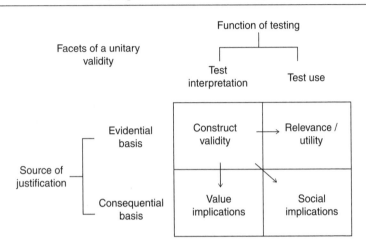

The consequential basis of the framework, which includes appraisal of value implications and social implications, is seen by some as a controversial departure from previous conceptions of validity. But Messick (1989) saw the examination of values inherent in construct names and theories as being within the scope of validity inquiry. For Messick, "the consequential basis of test interpretation is the appraisal of the value implications of the construct label, of the theory underlying the test interpretation, and of the ideologies in which the theory is embedded" (p. 20). He described "the consequential basis of test use [as] the appraisal of both potential and actual social consequences of the applied testing" (p. 20), adding a complex sociocultural layer to the validation process. Decades later, debate continues about the breadth of Messick's definition of validity (e.g., Cizek, 2012; Lissitz, 2009). There is no dispute, however, that value implications and social consequences are matters of importance in all testing and assessment and that Messick's treatment of these topics is seminal. Nevertheless, even as the 1999 *Standards* included consequences in the chapter on validity, some disagree that such issues should be encompassed in the meaning of validity, as noted in Chapter 3.

Messick (1989) expanded the scope of validation by incorporating constructs, test use, values, and consequences all into a validity framework. He explained the framework in terms of his analysis of the evolving philosophy of science that recognized the culturally and historically situated values guiding the process of validation. In view of the breadth and depth of this chapter, it has been recognized as a profound desideratum by some professionals and as a bewildering, erudite addition by others. Messick's presentation of validity has fueled rich reflection and debate in the field, but it has also added the complexity of social and cultural dimensions to the process of validation.

2006: Validity of Interpretation and Use

Kane's 2006 chapter in *Educational Measurement* defined validity by describing the action of validation: "to validate an interpretation or use of measurements is to evaluate the rationale, or argument, for the claims being made, and this in turn requires a clear statement of the proposed interpretations and uses and critical evaluation of these interpretations and uses" (p. 17). Whereas Messick had referred to interpretations and actions, Kane used the expression "interpretations and uses," which might be seen as narrower in scope. However, the more telling difference in Kane's presentation from that of Messick is the shift from the scientific language of empirical evidence and theoretical rationales to the language of rhetoric. Kane wrote about evaluating "the rationale, or argument for the claims" made about test interpretation and use. From a theoretical perspective, Messick had spanned the divide between the science of validation and the sociopolitical context of testing, but Kane went further by actually framing the validation process in its social context with multiple potential participants: "Ultimately, the need for validation derives from the scientific and social requirement that public claims and decisions be justified" (p. 17).

Kane's goal was to provide a pragmatic approach for doing validation as a means of putting into practice analytic frameworks such as Messick's for defining validity (Kane, 2001). Kane later reflected on the argument-based approach as a means of extending "the construct-validity model by substituting an IUA [interpretation/use argument] that specifies the inferences and assumptions inherent in the proposed interpretation and use of the test scores for the kind of scientific theory envisioned by Cronbach and Meehl (1955)" (Kane, 2016, p. 208). Kane's approach was to shift from positioning constructs as the basis for test score interpretation to requiring the tester to specify claims expressing the meaning of the score and the inferences required to make such claims. The useful insight accomplished by the shift from constructs to claims is that test interpretations and uses entail multiple different types of meanings, only some of which can be expressed by construct definitions. Moreover, it is up to the tester to formulate the relevant claims, depending on the intended meanings, and then to investigate the defensibility of the intended meanings for the intended users. This "contingent approach to validation," as Kane put it, has the advantage of

12

customizing the validation research program to meet the needs of the test users in their particular contexts of test use, rather than requiring all testing programs to engage in a prescribed process of validation (p. 208). In other words, a contingent approach is intended to recognize context-specific validation needs.

Kane's representation of validation as a process, as shown in Figure 1.4, consists of three types of actions. In the first, the test developer creates an interpretation/use argument that will serve "as the framework for collecting and presenting evidence" for the test score interpretation and use (Kane, 1992, p. 527). The rest of this book explains how interpretation/use arguments are constructed by assembling the intended claims about the test score interpretation and use into a logical structure, or chain, through the use of inferences. The second action is to design and carry out the research required to provide support for making the inferences that lead to each claim. The research can consist of documenting test development practices, expert analysis of content, statistical item analysis, theoretically motivated correlational analyses, and standard-setting research, for example. The research needed depends on the inferences and claims in the interpretation/ use argument. The third action is to summarize the research results in a validity argument. The validity argument states the claims and the rationales for their support, insofar as support is warranted on the basis of research results.

The central contribution of the argument-based approach is that it helps testers use the concepts introduced in previous definitions of validity to conceptualize a concrete process for conducting relevant research and interpreting its results. Despite the pragmatic goals of a validity argument framework, at first glance, concepts such as "inferences" and "claims" seem at least as abstract as those in previous frameworks. Especially for testers still thinking in terms of three validities, the conceptual leap into

Figure 1.4 Schematic Representation of the Process of Validation Based on Kane (2006)

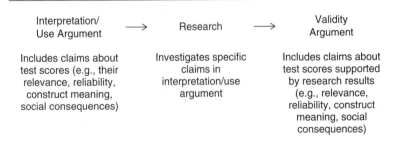

validity argument may seem daunting. The sketch of the academic background of the validity argument in this chapter provides some scaffolding because it introduces the central concepts in testing required for developing validity arguments.

Evolving Concepts in Testing

Concepts such as test performance, constructs, and values have been introduced and used in the successive chapters of *Educational Measurement* to conceptualize validity and validation, and these all remain important in argument-based validity. Seven such expressions are included in Table 1.1, each with a note about its respective role and degree of significance in each of the four presentations of validity from 1951 through 2006.

Cureton (1951) saw content as central to validity because both the relevance of a test and the selection of criterion performance depend on content. Cronbach (1971) did not dispute the importance of test content, in particular for its role in the operational definition of the construct and for descriptive interpretations of test scores, but he acknowledged the limitation of test content for explaining test scores. Even though Messick (1989) did not maintain the expression "content validity" in his unitary definition of validity, he recognized content-related evidence as important for investigating construct validity, which for him was central. Kane (2006) saw test content as relevant for inclusion in a validity argument because test tasks define the nature of the samples of performance that can provide one basis for score interpretations. Chapter 6 explains how the definition and selection of test content during the development process can be included in a validity argument to assert the role of test content in score interpretation. Chapter 4 offers a second avenue: Argument-based validity provides for inclusion of test content, with a claim that the score interpretation is relevant to the content of certain tasks in the classroom, curriculum, or real-world contexts.

Reliability has been seen as central to validity at least since the 1950s, when Cureton (1951) defined reliability as one of the two aspects of validity (see Figure 1.1) and demonstrated that the "validity coefficient" was limited by the reliability of both the test and the criterion measure. Cronbach (1971) also saw reliability as central to validity, but whereas Cureton emphasized the number of samples of performance, Cronbach focused on the consistency of the sample of performance obtained from test tasks developed from the operational definition. Messick (1989) built upon Cronbach's emphasis on the substantive interpretation of consistency by defining a construct as an interpretation of performance consistency. Accordingly, Kane (2006) created a means of making claims about reliability for inclusion in validity arguments, as described in Chapter 5.

Table 1.1 The Roles of Testing Concepts in Four Editions of *Educational Measurement* (1951–2006)

Aspects of testing	*Edition of Educational Measurement*			
	1951: Validity of a test	*1971: Validity of interpretations*	*1989: Validity of interpretations and actions*	*2006: Validity of interpretation and use*
Test content	Critical to relevance (one aspect of validity); must be demonstrably relevant to criterion performance	Important for interpretations required for validation (content validity); part of the operational definition, which is critical to validation	Key to content evidence for validity as one source of evidence to be used when investigating score meaning	Relevant for interpretations about the quality of the test tasks and about the appropriateness of scores for particular uses
Reliability	One of the two aspects of validity and required to obtain a high "validity coefficient"	Important because it is connected to the operational definition (which must be consistent across test tasks) and the construct (based on consistent categories)	Central to validation because performance consistency is summarized and expressed by test scores	One interpretation that can be made based on test scores; if it is made, it must be included in the argument
Performance	Central to both aspects of validity: Relevance requires a sample of performance to represent a defined universe of behavior; reliability requires a sample of performance of sufficient size	The critical result of a good operational definition	The consistency in performance is critical for score interpretation	A legitimate source of meaning for score interpretation; if it is used to express the score meaning, it must be specified in the argument

Construct	Not given any role	Introduced as critical to validation because it identifies the categories created to interpret test scores	The foundation for the validity framework and basis for a unitary definition	One interpretation that can be made based on test scores; if made, it must be included in the argument
Test use	Not central to validity; recognized as creating a dilemma for testers because of the limits of validation research	One of the two types of validity investigations focusing on usefulness for decision making	Central to validity definition: interpretations and actions; "test use" is an action performed with test scores	A critical part of an argument for interpretation and use
Values	Not central to validity, but limitations of criterion measures and users' pressing needs for tests create a value-laden dilemma for responsible professionals	The basis for professional responsibility of testers to pursue a rigorous program of scientific hypothesis testing and for decision making	Critical to the validity framework, which includes "values" as they connect with both construct meaning and consequences of testing	Inherent in the validation process; can be specified as assumptions underlying their respective inferences in a validity argument
Consequences	Not central to validity, but prompts recognition of the limits of validation research for contributing to desired social consequences	The source of concerns about effects on students when tests are used in educational decision making	Critical to the validity framework, which includes "consequences" of testing	The cause for public engagement, which motivates the need for validity arguments

Performance is treated as central to both of Cureton's (1951) aspects of validity: Reliability requires a sample of performance of sufficient size, and relevance requires the sample of performance to represent a defined universe of behavior. The latter requirement makes performance integral to defining score meaning in the absence of constructs. Cronbach (1971) did not require performance to serve as a basis for score interpretation, but, for him, eliciting relevant performance was nevertheless integral to validation. Messick (1989) amplified the relative roles Cronbach placed on performance and constructs by relying on constructs as the basis for the meaning of test scores and defining the construct as a meaningful interpretation of performance consistency, rather than simply an interpretation of performance. If Cronbach and Messick appeared to de-emphasize the role of performance in score interpretation, Kane (2006) opened the door for re-emphasizing it. Performance is viewed by Kane as a legitimate source of meaning for score interpretation in a validity argument. He therefore places on the table for consideration by testers both the performance-oriented view of score interpretation presented by Cureton and the construct-oriented view of Cronbach and Messick. Chapter 4 explains how one or both of these approaches can be expressed in argument-based validity.

Constructs have been the aspect of validation whose role has had the most dramatic metamorphosis. Cureton's account of validity in 1951 did not even mention constructs. Cronbach (1971) included constructs as critical to validation because they identify the categories created to interpret test scores, and Messick (1989) considered constructs central to validity inquiry. Kane (2006) presented constructs as one way of expressing score interpretation but not the only way the substantive meaning of scores can be expressed. Chapter 4 explains how testers can formulate a validity argument with or without a theoretical construct.

Test use in terms of placement, selection, certification, or grading was not central to Cureton's (1951) definition of validity. He defined relevance, one aspect of validity, with reference to the behaviors or criterion measures in the domain of interest, rather than as relevance for decision making in educational, clinical, and work settings. For him, validity had to be for a particular purpose, but ironically, he defined purpose as what is tested and who is tested, but not what for. In fact, Cureton saw test use as creating a challenge for testers because of the limits of validation research. Cronbach (1971), in contrast, included test use for decision making in his validity framework (see Figure 1.2.). He depicted studies of specific decision-making uses of tests as one way of investigating validity, but he stopped short of defining validity as pertaining to both interpretations and uses. Messick (1989) took the additional step of including test use by defining validity as a judgment about the interpretations and actions based on test scores. Test use is an action performed with test scores in a particular social and cultural context, and therefore evidence of the relevance and utility are required to make a validity judgment. Kane (2006) defined validity as an appraisal of the rationale for test interpretation and use. In doing so, he strengthened the imperative for a validity argument to take into account the sociocultural context of test use. Accordingly, Chapter 3 demonstrates how to include test use in a validity argument.

Values underlying validation research are evident throughout the four chapters, although their prominence and roles shift. Values are expressed in Cureton's (1951) and Cronbach's (1971) depictions of a community of testers guided by their earnest professionalism as they attempt to provide well-justified advice to test users. Cureton acknowledged that the definition of validity requiring a perfect criterion measure created a moral dilemma in view of both the need to advise prospective test users about validity and the impossibility of doing so because of insufficient criterion measures. Despite Cronbach's framing of validation in scientific terms, he recognized that values and judgments were integral to a never-ending validation process propelled by the ethical pursuit of defensible test interpretations. He also saw values as the basis of decision making, regardless of the statistical data analysis serving in the process.

Messick (1989) included values explicitly in his validity framework (see Figure 1.3.) with an extensive discussion of value implications. In particular, Messick pointed out the implicit cultural and political values concealed in constructs such as "intelligence" and "aptitude" in the first half of the 1900s. Gould's (1996) analysis shows how the racist values of this time period formed the basis for intelligence research and how the tests were used to perpetuate these values. Zwick (2006) summarizes the foundation of modern college admissions testing in the northeastern United States at a time when 2% of the population attended college and three-quarters of them were white men. Values instituted in these tests were arguably exclusionary, even though today similar practices are intended to implement the values of an inclusive, merit-based system. The historical shift may partially explain today's irony that, as Zwick points out, "to some, tests like the SAT are harsh and capricious gatekeepers that bar the road to advancement; to others, they are the gateways to opportunity" (p. 649).

Kane (2006) further shifted the role and meaning of values for validation by explaining how they extend beyond the community of testers working on a particular testing issue to responsibility for communicating the logic of the validity argument. In a sense, the raison d'être of argument-based validity is to have sufficient technical language to develop the logic behind test use so that a rationale can be judged by others for its soundness and evaluated for its relevance to other test takers and other contexts. In short, today values are recognized to permeate all aspects of the validation process—as illustrated in Cizek's (2012) revision of Messick's (1989) characterization of the validation process—and are therefore relevant to every chapter.

The social consequences of testing were recognized by Cureton (1951), who wrote about the limits of validation research for serving society, with recommendations about the validity of tests for such purposes as career guidance, qualifications certification, and educational advancement. Cronbach's (1971) discussion of decision making as one of the two types of investigations for validity inquiry is concerned with school-based consequences, which included concerns about effects on students. Cronbach's highly social and political treatment of validity appeared much later (Cronbach, 1988), when he introduced the need for validity arguments that speak to a variety of audiences. Messick (1989) placed social consequences within his validity framework, and influenced by Messick, the *Standards* included "evidence based on consequences of tests" (p. 30) as one type of validity evidence. Building on Cronbach's 1988 positioning of validity argument in the social and political context, validity argument provides a mechanism for inclusion of consequences, as explained in Chapter 3. The relationship between testers and society from the early 1950s into the 2000s reflects a change in perspective from educational and psychological testing as a neutral science to its conception today as a culturally situated social responsibility. As a result, today the fairness of test interpretation and use for individuals and subgroups within the population are areas of continuing analysis and research, which take into account the consequences of testing (Camilli, 2006).

Conclusion

The basic testing concepts introduced over the past decades remain useful for understanding and developing validity arguments today. Moreover, the chronology of definitions of validity and validation in the field should enable readers to see both the complexity of validation issues and the variation in how they can be conceived. Like the history outlined in this chapter, the academic discussion of validity argument continues (e.g., see the papers by Brennan, Haertel, Moss, and Sireci in the *Journal of Educational Measurement*, 2013). Despite the value of the continuing academic discussion about the epistemological frameworks (e.g., Lissitz, 2009; Moss, 1994) and methods underlying professional conceptions of validity, in the real world of testing practice, professionals need to be able to justifying test score interpretations and uses. As Shepard (1993) pointed out, understanding validation is cultivated, in part, through the study of examples of actual validation practices. Examples of argument-based validity in practice, however, are rare, meaning that the academic discussion of validity argument is undertaken largely in the abstract. This book is intended to expand the circle of professionals able to use argument-based validity for designing and conducting research on tests used for a range of purposes. Most professionals and students of testing are familiar with the basic concepts, if not their history, as introduced in this chapter. The following chapters will build on them to explain how testers can construct their own validity arguments.

Chapter 2

VALIDITY ARGUMENT DESIGN

The *Standards* presents validation as an evidence-based process of developing and evaluating arguments about the interpretation and use of test scores. It states, "Decisions about what types of evidence are important for the validation argument in each instance can be clarified by developing a set of propositions or claims that support the proposed interpretation for the particular purpose of testing" (AERA et al., 2014, p. 12). In view of the multifaceted interpretations and uses that need to be taken into account in validation, a comprehensive, systematic approach to generating propositions is needed. In Kane's (1992) terms, validation efforts need to focus "attention on the details of the interpretation" (p. 527). This chapter introduces how the details of interpretation and use are taken into account in argument-based validity, as presented by Kane (e.g., 1992, 2001, 2006, 2013). It begins by introducing three tests that will serve as examples throughout the book. These tests provide concrete examples of how claims and inferences are used to express the meanings that make up their respective score interpretations and uses, how the claims serve as connectors in multipart arguments, as well as how argument-based validity provides the tools for specifying the evidence required to develop and evaluate a validity argument.

Expressing Interpretations and Uses: Three Example Tests

Three example tests were selected to represent three different contexts and test uses. Each was developed within the academic traditions of validation research outlined in Chapter 1, even though only one, the Test of English as a Foreign Language Internet-Based Test (TOEFL iBT), has had a Kane-style validity argument developed to support its interpretation and use. First published in 2005, the TOEFL iBT is a test of academic English proficiency intended primarily to aid in university admissions decisions for applicants whose first language is not English. The TOEFL iBT is the most recent version in a tradition begun in the 1960s of developing and administering a test for use in admissions decisions at North American universities. Published by Educational Testing Service, an established research and development organization in the United States, the TOEFL iBT has been the subject of years of validation research. Although research continues to be published in journal articles and research reports by Educational Testing Service, in the mid-2000s results were summarized in a book that presents the validity argument for the intended interpretations and uses of the TOEFL iBT (Chapelle, Enright, & Jamieson, 2008).

The second example is the Mayer-Salovey-Caruso Emotional Intelligence Test (MSCEIT), a test of emotional intelligence that was developed by psychologists and published by MHS Assessments for use in a range of settings in which intellectual capacities for perceiving emotions and reasoning about them are of interest to score users. Research on emotional intelligence dates back decades, leaving a trail of research articles in major academic journals in psychology, some of which are about the MSCEIT and its development. The published research provides the large majority of the publicly available information about the test (Mayer, Caruso, & Salovey, 2016; Mayer, Salovey, & Caruso, 2008).

The third example is the mathematics section of the Iowa Assessments (University of Iowa, 2015), which is intended to assess the mathematics skills of students taught in the public school curriculum from kindergarten through Grade 12 in the United States. The Iowa Assessments are a product of decades of research and development at the University of Iowa. The information presented about the Iowa Assessments comes from the *Research and Development Guide: Iowa Assessments, Forms E and F* (University of Iowa, 2015), which contains references to journal articles reporting additional research. Intended for scores users, the *Research and Development Guide* explains the development, basis for validity claims, and ongoing analysis of test results.

As tests developed by professionals, all three produce scores that have been shown to be reliable, and therefore various types of reliability claims have appeared in the reports about the tests. However, reliability claims do not encompass all of the meanings entailed in the score interpretations and uses. For each of the three tests, Table 2.1 shows an example of another claim about each of the test scores, the meaning it conveys about the test scores, and the inference required to attribute the meaning to the test scores. Argument-based validity provides for all claims made about test scores to express the detail of the test interpretation and use.

One of the claims about the TOEFL iBT scores is that they are relevant to the quality of linguistic performance in English-medium universities. The test developers make this claim because they have designed the test to assess academic language proficiency rather than general language proficiency or language proficiency in another domain such as tourism, mechanics, or business. This claim is important for the TOEFL iBT users because they recognize that the language demands in higher education require certain types of performance: Students need to use English to learn new concepts, critically analyze what they read and hear, and express their

Table 2.1 Three Example Tests, Claims About Their Score Meaning, Types of Meanings, and Inferences Required to Attribute Meaning

Test	Claim About Test Scores	Meaning Attributed to Test Scores	Inference Required to Attribute Meaning
Academic English: TOEFL iBT	TOEFL iBT scores are relevant to the quality of linguistic performance in English-medium universities.	Real-world relevance	Extrapolation
Emotional intelligence: MSCEIT	Scores reflect the ability to recognize and reason about emotions.	Substantive sense	Explanation
Mathematics achievement test: Iowa Assessments	Iowa Assessments are useful for educational purposes requiring descriptive data on an individual student or groups of students.	Functional role	Utilization

knowledge and analyses. English-language tests are not all equally suited to assess academic language, and therefore they would not be relevant to performance at a university. By interpreting the test scores as relevant to language performance in English-medium academic contexts, test users make an extrapolation inference. This means that they are using the score on the test to extrapolate, or extend beyond, the known test score to the unknown judgments about test takers' language performance in an English-medium university.

One of the claims about the MSCEIT is that its scores reflect test takers' ability to recognize and reason about emotions. This is a claim about the construct, or substantive sense, of the scores because it gives the score meaning with respect to the knowledge, skills, and abilities that the test is intended to assess. The construct label *emotional intelligence* is a shorthand descriptive name for the substantive sense, but that label alone is not sufficiently precise to express the substantive meaning of the test score interpretation. A number of tests are referred to as tests of emotional intelligence, but they do not all actually assess the cognitive aspects of recognition and reasoning, so making a specific claim about the intended score meaning in addition to the label of emotional intelligence is important. When test users interpret the test scores as having the substantive sense of recognizing and reasoning about emotions, they make an explanation inference. In other words, they are accepting that the ability to recognize and reason about emotions explains the test scores, and the explanation comes from a psychological definition of the capacity (Mislevy, 2006).

One of the claims about the Iowa Assessments mathematics achievement test scores is that they are useful for "a variety of important educational purposes that involve the collection and use of information describing either an individual student or groups of students" (University of Iowa, 2015, p. 3). The claim about the intended role of the scores gives them a functional meaning by indicating what they should be used for. A test of mathematics would be designed differently if results were intended to be used for college admissions or certified public accountant (CPA) licensure, for example. The *Research and Development Guide* (University of Iowa, 2015) explains the functional role in more detail by stating types of school-based decisions that the scores are intended to support. For a mathematics test designed for college admissions or licensure, statements about the functional role would refer to decision making for institutions and for society rather than decision making for students. The inference required for putting the test scores to use for a particular purpose is utilization.

Using Claims and Inferences to Express Interpretations and Uses

The claims shown for each of the example tests illustrate what Kane (1992) meant by "the details of the interpretation" (p. 527). Claims express the types of meanings intended when test scores are interpreted. The term *claim* refers to a statement that is made about the test scores, including various aspects of their qualities, meanings, and intended impacts. The term *claim* is used instead of *fact* because a claim is a statement that is open to dispute and, therefore, typically requires evidence supporting its credibility. For each of the example claims in Table 2.1, the research conducted on the respective test has offered some support for the claim. Because claims attribute meaning to test scores on the basis of evidence, they act as conclusions drawn by making inferences. "Inference" in argument-based validity refers to the process of drawing conclusions about score meaning.

To use argument-based validity, therefore, a tester needs to be able to render intended score meanings (i.e., interpretations and uses) as claims that serve as conclusions for certain inferences. Table 2.2 summarizes four

24

Table 2.2   Four Meanings Attributed to Test Scores, General Claims, and Inferences Leading to Their Respective Claims

Meaning Attributed to Test Scores	General Claim	Inference Leading to the Claim: Definition
Real-world relevance	Test scores are based on performance on test tasks relevant to the context of interest.	Extrapolation: The score user accepts that the score meaning extends to the context of interest.
Substantive sense	The test scores reflect the intended construct.	Explanation: The score user surmises that the score meaning is explained by the defined construct.
Functional role	The test scores are useful for their stated purpose.	Utilization: The score user trusts that the scores should be used for the stated purpose.
Degree of stability	The test produces reliable scores.	Generalization: The score user concludes that the test produces reliable scores.

aspects of test score meaning along with claims that are stated in general terms and, for each claim, the type of inference that would be made if the claim were accepted.

The example claim for the TOEFL iBT academic English test in Table 2.1 illustrated one way of expressing a claim about the real-world relevance of the test score. Generally speaking, the claim is that test scores are based on test performance relevant to the context of interest. Such a claim attributes meaning to the scores in terms of the congruity of the test tasks with tasks that people do in the real world and, in particular, in the context of interest to score users. Such a claim gives the test scores a vivid meaning to many score users who can see the connection between what the test taker was required to do on the test and what they have to do in the real world. Kane, Crooks, and Cohen (1999) emphasized that accepting such a claim requires the score user to be able to extrapolate from the test score to performance in a particular context of interest, and the inference is therefore referred to as extrapolation.

The example claim about the substantive sense of the MSCEIT is that scores reflect the test takers' ability to recognize and reason about emotions. The general claim is that the test scores reflect the intended construct, which is typically expressed as the knowledge, skills, and abilities required for performance. As Messick (1989) put it, constructs are meaningful interpretations of performance consistency. The ability to troubleshoot computer failures, proficiency in speaking French, and knowledge of multiplication tables are examples of constructs. Constructs are not observed directly. It must be surmised that the score meaning is explained by the defined construct. The inference is therefore called explanation.

The example claim about the functional role of the mathematics subtest of the Iowa Assessments is that the scores are useful for educational purposes requiring information that describes individuals or groups of students. Generally speaking, the claim is that the scores are useful for their stated purpose. Purposes can include the range of functions that tests are created to serve such as certification, placement, and diagnosis. As Cureton (1951) emphasized, the purpose also includes the test takers for whom the stated uses are intended. When score users trust that the scores should be used for their stated purpose, they are making a utilization inference.

Claims about reliability attribute the scores with a meaning about their degree of stability, or consistency. *Consistency* can refer to the stability of scores across different forms and occasions of testing. It can indicate consistency across tasks on the test, meaning that the score reflects multiple samples of performance that are justifiably combined into one score. Consistency can also refer to consistent judgments of multiple raters across their ratings or occasions of rating. In other words, reliability encompasses multiple different types of consistencies, each of which is estimated in a different way.

The following chapters examine these claims and inferences in more detail and introduce some additional ones. But for this chapter, these four types of claims provide a basis for understanding the tools required for structuring claims into arguments and identifying the evidence required to support them.

Structuring Claims in a Validity Argument:
From Grounds to Conclusions

For any test, more than a single claim is made to express the score interpretation and use, so validation is never a single study for investigating one claim. Instead, multiple claims with their inferences are structured together into what Cronbach (1988) called a "validity argument": Based on the idea that validation is evaluation, Cronbach suggested that "what House (1977) has called 'the logic of evaluation argument' applies," and he invited testers to "think of 'validity argument' rather than validation research" (Cronbach, 1988, p. 4).

Cronbach saw a validity argument as having a political dimension because it provides a means of integrating multiple meanings of test scores for diverse audiences. Kane (1992) developed argument-based validity from a more technical standpoint, as a practical argument supported by incomplete or even questionable evidence. Practical arguments are never proven; they are "at best, convincing or plausible" (p. 527). Kane structured claims and inferences into an argument by drawing upon Toulmin's (2003) argument structure that begins with a premise, or grounds, and ends with a conclusion. An inference makes the connection, or link, from the grounds to the conclusion. Applying this argument structure to testing, Figure 2.1 illustrates how the claim about the substantive meaning of the scores for the MSCEIT serves as a conclusion for the explanation inference. The premise is the test scores, and an explanation inference leads to the conclusion that the scores reflect the test takers' ability to recognize and reason about emotions. In this argument, the claim serves as the conclusion.

To develop Figure 2.1 into a more complete argument, the basic three-part structure needs to be expanded to accommodate additional claims and inferences. Figure 2.2 illustrates how this is done by adding a claim about reliability and a generalization inference. Figure 2.2 again shows the test scores as the premise, or grounds. The first inference, generalization, leads to the conclusion that the test produces reliable scores. This conclusion also serves as the premise for the explanation inference, which leads to the conclusion that the scores reflect the test takers' ability to recognize and reason about emotions. This illustrates how a validity argument structure strands together premise–inference–conclusion sequences in which the conclusion from one valid inference serves as the premise for the next. This example

Figure 2.1 Structure of an Argument About Test Scores for the MSCEIT Serving as a Premise for an Explanation Inference that Concludes the Scores Reflect the Test Takers' Ability to Recognize and Reason About Emotions

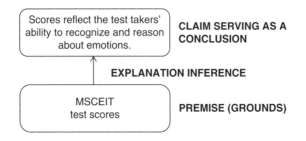

Figure 2.2   Structure of an Argument About Test Scores for the MSCEIT
With a Premise (Grounds) and Inferences Leading to Two
Logically Related Claims About Reliability and Constructs

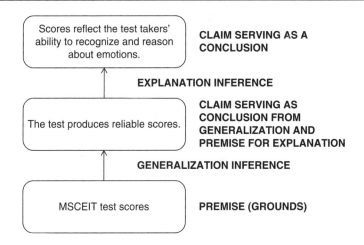

also shows a notation for expressing Cronbach's and Messick's view that a construct interpretation can be made only if scores are shown to be reliable: The reliable scores are the grounds for the explanation inference.

A second example of a chain of claims appears in Figure 2.3, which illustrates the logic behind the claim about the usefulness of the scores on the Iowa Assessments mathematics section. The test scores are the premise or grounds. The first inference leads to the conclusion that the test scores are based on performance on tasks relevant to actual situations in which students use math skills. This conclusion also serves as the premise for the utilization inference, and the utilization inference leads to the final conclusion, the claim that the Iowa Assessments mathematics scores provide information to aid in decision making for students.

Validity arguments typically have more claims and inferences than those shown in Figures 2.2 and 2.3, but these examples should suffice to demonstrate the validity argument figures in this book, which uses the metaphor of grounds to place the premise at the bottom of the argument diagrams. The figures in this book are consistent with many of the publications about validity argument, but one can also find ample examples of argument diagrams that place the premises to the left of their respective inferences and conclusions. The left-to-right reading of such diagrams has the same meaning as the corresponding bottom-to-top reading of the diagrams in this book.

Figure 2.3 Structure of an Argument About Test Scores for the Iowa
Assessments Mathematics Achievement Test, Including the
Test Scores as Premise (Grounds) and Inferences Leading
to Two Logically Related Claims About Relevance and
Test Use

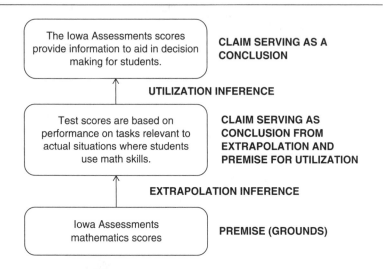

Each of the four claims appearing in Figures 2.2 and 2.3 is about the
specific score interpretation for one of the example tests. To summarize the
structuring of claims and inferences in more general terms, Table 2.3 presents the premises, inferences, and general claims for the generic versions
of these argument structures and the meaning that each inference adds to
the scores.

When the scores serve as the premise or grounds for the first inference,
they are typically stated as a phrase, for example, "Iowa Assessments mathematics scores." The grounds for the following inferences, however, are
conclusions from the previous inferences (e.g., "Test scores are based on
performance on tasks relevant to actual situations in which students use
math skills."). Conclusions are often restated as claims, which are full sentences; although, when considered as grounds, such conclusions can be
restated as phrases, too. For example, the conclusion "Test scores are based
on performance on tasks relevant to actual situations in which students use
math skills" can be restated as grounds with the expression "relevant math
skills." The recognition of the statement/phrase form of claims in a
validity argument is useful for reading academic articles on validity
argument because they often use shorthand expressions in validity argument diagrams to represent conclusions and premises. Instead of the

relatively transparent expressions such as "reliable scores" and "relevant scores," they also use expressions such as "expected scores" and "target scores." The use of these technical terms in place of the complete sentences used to express claims is a useful shorthand device, but only if they are understood. The four core meanings of test scores can be expressed with the claims and inferences exemplified in Table 2.2, but other inferences entailed in test score interpretation express variations of the core meanings, as well. These will be introduced in the following chapters to bring the total to seven inferences. But argument-based validity is not conceived as a fixed list of inferences. Instead, the intent is to provide the conceptual tools and language to help test developers and researchers to identify inferences that are important in their specific test interpretations and uses. A validity argument for a particular test "should reflect the proposed interpretation and use; it should not be constrained to fit some predefined structure" (Kane, 2013, p. 10).

Table 2.3 General Claims With Their Grounds and Inferences

Figure	Meaning	Premise (Grounds)	Inference	General Claim
Figure 2.2	Degree of stability	Test scores	Generalization	The test produces reliable scores.
	Substantive sense	The test produces reliable scores.	Explanation	The test scores reflect the intended construct.
Figure 2.3	Real-world relevance	Test scores	Extrapolation	Test scores are based on performance on test tasks relevant to the context of interest.
	Functional role	Test scores are based on performance on test tasks relevant to the context of interest.	Utilization	The scores are useful for their intended purpose.

Nevertheless, the four inferences introduced so far demonstrate how some of the basic constituents are combined to sketch the structure for an argument.

Identifying Evidence: Warrants, Assumptions, and Backing

The example arguments outlined above would be the beginning of what Kane (2013) calls an "interpretation/use argument." To develop interpretation/ use arguments into validity arguments, evidence is needed to support each of the inferences leading to its respective claim. In order to identify the types of evidence that would serve in support, more detail is needed. In validity arguments, the detail is expressed in warrants and assumptions.

Kane (2013) defined a warrant as a statement that expresses a "rule for inferring claims of a certain kind from data of a certain kind" (p. 12). Warrants are thought of as allowing, authorizing, or licensing inferences. They do so by first adding precision to the meaning of inferences. For example, an explanation inference allows for an interpretation about the substantive construct meaning of the test score, but what does that imply for the validation research needed for the emotional intelligence test? Construct validation can entail a full range of research methodologies, as suggested by the five sources of evidence identified in the *Standards*. Warrants need to serve in formulating specific research goals whose results may support the inferences in the validity argument.

Table 2.4 provides examples of the types of warrants that could be used to license the inferences leading to the claims about scores on the tests. The extrapolation inference leading to the claim that the academic English TOEFL iBT scores are relevant to the quality of linguistic performance in English-medium universities has a warrant that adds to the inference: "The construct of academic language proficiency as assessed by the TOEFL iBT accounts for the quality of linguistic performance in English-medium institutions of higher education" (Chapelle et al., 2008, p. 348). Support for this warrant will require research that investigates the relationship between the TOEFL scores and other criterion scores that are indicators of aspects of academic language proficiency and linguistic performance in higher education.

Which criterion measures should be accepted as relevant and what kind of relationships should be expected require still another level of detail, which should be built into the validity argument by adding assumptions underlying each of the warrants. Assumptions underlying this warrant in the TOEFL validity argument name specific types of criterion measures, including test takers' self-assessments, professor's judgments, and scores

Table 2.4 Example Claims, Inferences, and Warrants in
Validity Arguments

Claim	Inference Leading to Claim	Example Warrant Licensing the Inference
TOEFL iBT scores are relevant to the quality of linguistic performance in English-medium universities.	Extrapolation	The construct of academic language proficiency as assessed by the TOEFL iBT accounts for the quality of linguistic performance in English-medium institutions of higher education (Chapelle et al., 2008, p. 348).
MSCEIT scores reflect the ability to recognize and reason about emotions.	Explanation	Test scores support the theorized four-component model of emotional intelligence that includes managing emotions to attain specific goals, understanding emotions and emotional language and signals, using emotions to facilitate thinking, and perceiving emotions accurately in oneself and in others (Mayer et al., 2016).
The Iowa Assessments scores provide information to aid in decision making for students.	Utilization	The scores can "identify strengths and weaknesses in student performance—make relative comparisons of student performance from one content area to another" (University of Iowa, 2015, p. 3).

on another academic English test. Assumptions are examined for the extrapolation inference in Chapter 4, and for all seven inferences in the following chapters, but suffice it to say in this chapter that well-written warrants and assumptions can pinpoint the research required to support a particular inference by identifying the empirically testable hypotheses.

The explanation inference about the construct of the MSCEIT scores needs a warrant that specifies in greater detail the meaning of the construct. The warrant would be that test scores support the theorized four-component model of emotional intelligence that includes managing emotions to attain specific goals, understanding emotions and emotional language and signals, using emotions to facilitate thinking, and perceiving emotions accurately in oneself and in others (Mayer et al., 2016). Chapter 4 shows how such a warrant about the construct is used to develop more specific assumptions about, for example, the hypothesized degree of relationship among the four components of the model and their place in a larger nomothetic network of subconstructs of intelligence. These assumptions, in turn, point to the types of research required to support the warrant. If research results are indeed supportive, the results serve as backing for the warrant, which authorizes the inference leading to its conclusion that the test assesses emotional intelligence.

The third example shown in Table 2.4 is the utilization inference leading to the claim that the Iowa Assessments mathematics scores provide information to aid in decision making for students. The warrants authorizing such an inference would state the intended uses of the test scores and the rules for specific score-based decisions. Assumptions would identify the findings needed to make the warrants credible.

Warrants such as those illustrated in Table 2.4 add detail to the meaning of inferences in validity arguments, but additional detail is needed to specify research questions. Assumptions provide detail that suggests types of evidence that need to be found through research. In the validity argument, such evidence is "backing" for assumptions because certain pieces of evidence serve as support for making particular assumptions. Assumptions and backing obviously have to get deeply into the detail of validation for specific tests and are, therefore, illustrated further in the following chapters.

Identifying Weaknesses and Limitations in Arguments: Rebuttals

The claims, inferences, warrants, and assumptions illustrated earlier are all used to state the intended interpretations and uses of test scores. These are the primary concern for test developers wanting to present a validity argument supporting their test's interpretation and use. But they do not fully serve Cronbach's (1971) view of validation as scientific hypothesis testing, which requires a means of expressing threats to the intended interpretations, or "rival hypotheses that may challenge the proposed interpretation" (AERA et al., 2014, p. 12). In some cases, threats to intended interpretations need to be identified and investigated for certain individuals or groups. In the *Standards* (Chapter 3), such threats to validity are treated as concerns about test fairness. In validity arguments, threats are expressed at the level of individual inferences, to isolate the specific source of hypothesized unfairness within the complex chain of inferences entailed in the intended interpretation and use. Hypothesized threats to validity for all test takers, or for certain individuals and groups, are expressed in argument-based validity with rebuttals.

A rebuttal in a validity argument states the conditions under which a particular warrant would not be able to license its respective inference, as illustrated in Table 2.5. For example, a rebuttal added to the claim in

Table 2.5 General Claims With Examples of Corresponding Warrants and Potential Rebuttals

General Claim (Inference)	Warrant	Potential Rebuttals
Test scores are based on performance on test tasks relevant to the context of interest. (Extrapolation)	The test tasks elicit test takers' performance that reflects their performance in situations of interest to test score users.	• The important characteristics of tasks of interest to test users were not adequately analyzed. • The test takers have experience different from that of the group used to norm the test and are unfamiliar with the task content.
The test produces reliable scores. (Generalization)	A sufficient number of test tasks are given to test takers to produce reliable scores.	• Test administration is not carried out as specified in some locations. • The internal consistency reliability of the scores is different across different subgroups of the population.
The test measures the intended construct. (Explanation)	Test scores support the theorized internal structure of the construct the test is intended to measure.	• Some individuals are advantaged due to coaching on test content and format. • The test-taking processes are ineffective for some individuals whose first language is not English.
The scores are useful for their intended purpose. (Utilization)	The scores are appropriate for making decisions about mastery of the content covered in class.	• Test users do not obtain test results in a timely fashion. • Test content disproportionately favors students who have attended the same school for several years.

the second row about reliability would read, "It can be concluded that scores are reliable because support was found for the assumptions underlying the warrant that a sufficient number of test tasks are given to test takers to produce reliable scores, unless it is also found that test administration is not carried out as specified in some locations." Rebuttals invite research to investigate the extent to which evidence supports them.

The examples in Table 2.5 show that rebuttals can be used to express what may go wrong in certain situations to weaken a validity argument. They can include cultural aspects of the setting that are different from those assumed by the test developer, test takers whose background is different from what is needed, a school situation in which the results cannot be acted upon as intended by the tester, and any number of other situation-specific and person-specific factors that potentially make test interpretation and use invalid. Rebuttals provide a heuristic for specifying testing practices likely to disproportionately affect a certain group of test takers or an individual with particular characteristics. In this way, rebuttals provide a means of including some of the fairness issues of interpretations and uses of test scores for decision making for certain individuals and groups, including those defined by demographics such as gender, race, and cultural background (Camilli, 2006; Xi, 2012).

If supported, rebuttals undermine the inferential process that the validity argument builds with claims, inferences, warrants, and assumptions. They are, therefore, useful tools for critics conducting evaluations of validity arguments developed by others, prospective test users wanting to evaluate test use for a different context, and test developers needing to identify areas requiring attention during test development. Disadvantages can typically be identified for certain groups of individuals, such as those with hearing or sight impairment, limited proficiency in the language of the test, or lack of experience with use of technology for testing. In these cases, accommodations need to be created to provide access for those individuals (*Standards,* Chapter 3). Even though test developers tend to focus on seeking support for claims and inferences, credible claims require the absence of support for rebuttals as well. Test developers, therefore, can use rebuttals to be proactive by identifying potential limits to the inferences and taking action by stating the limits on test use for certain groups and providing accommodations for other groups.

The Language of Validity Argument

Working with validity arguments requires testers to learn some new terms and ways of framing interpretation and use. Even though the claims, inferences, warrants, and assumptions express the same basic inferential processes that have been used for decades in testing research, at first glance, these terms seem puzzling to many testers. Many testers working on validation use the language of "types of evidence" from Messick's (1989) presentation of the faceted unitary validity, which is reflected in the *Standards*. However, neither Messick nor the *Standards* develop the specific language and logic for crafting the claims and specifying their roles in the interpretation and use of a particular test. The *Standards* refers to score interpretation and use, the associated propositions or claims to be supported, and the five types of evidence, but in practice, these three pieces are difficult for test developers and researchers to generate and stitch together. The result is reports of validity research with vague or unstated interpretations, incomplete or absent propositions, and research presented without an explanation of its contribution to a validity argument. What is missing in a "types of evidence" approach to validation is a systematic way of expressing the validity argument that Cronbach (1988) invited testers to think of.

Expressing the argument requires some additional terms beyond propositions, claims, and evidence. Table 2.6 shows the correspondence between the terms used in the *Standards* and those a validity argument framework provides to test developers and researchers. The terms are arranged in descending levels of generality from top to bottom, with the three levels of analysis in the *Standards* on the left, the seven levels used in validity arguments in the middle, and the definitions of the terms on the right. The argument-based approach prompts the test developer to elaborate the test's interpretation and use by analyzing the intended score meanings, specify the meanings with claims, identify the inference that leads to each claim, and use the claims and inferences to structure an argument. The tester then needs to provide additional detail using warrants that authorize the inferences and assumptions that provide still more specificity about the research to be conducted to make the warrants credible. Results from research motivated by specific assumptions in the validity argument can be interpreted with respect to the corresponding inference. These terms provide the detail required to express all aspects of score interpretation and use in a manner that motivates particular validation research and provides a context for its interpretation. The terms, therefore, allow testers not only to think of validity argument but also to express validity arguments to make clear the role of validity evidence.

36

Table 2.6 Terms Used for Expressing Validity Arguments, Arranged by Their Levels of Generality

	Standards	Validity Argument	Definitions
General	Interpretation and Use	Interpretation and Use	Overall statement of test purpose
		Score Meanings	General expressions denoting aspects of meaning
	Propositions (Claims)	Claims	General statements about interpretation and use
		Inferences	General technical terms denoting the steps in reasoning
		Warrants*	Statements indicating an inference can be authorized in a particular context
		Assumptions	Statements clarifying what evidence is needed
Specific	Evidence	Backing	Statements, paragraphs, tables, figures in extended descriptions of findings

*Note: Rebuttals are the statements corresponding to warrants that indicate conditions under which an inference cannot be authorized in a particular context.

Conclusion

The validity argument framework presented in this chapter provides a means for testers to state the details of test interpretation and use by analyzing intended score meanings. Four basic meanings of test scores can be expressed as claims, which serve as conclusions for particular inferences. Four terms—warrant, assumption, backing, and rebuttal—were introduced to show how the support for inferences is conceived and challenged in ways that point to specific validation research. In the following chapters, the four components of interpretation and use will be expanded into a more nuanced palette of meanings with additional claims, warrants, and assumptions. The next chapter shows that the functional role of a test can be expressed in terms of claims about test uses (e.g., achievement, prediction, diagnosis) and about specific decisions to be taken based on certain scores. The functional role can also be expressed as claims about consequences of test use on test takers, academic fields of study, or society. In this way, each chapter helps to expand the vocabulary of testing professionals for developing their own arguments about the validity of test interpretation and use.

Chapter 3

USES AND CONSEQUENCES OF TEST SCORES

This chapter explains how argument-based validity takes into account the functional role that test scores play in decision making and the consequences of their use. Examples of score-based decisions are admitting an applicant to a university, certifying a candidate's suitability to perform a particular job, placing a student at a certain level in a program of study, or planning a student's future instruction. Validation requires testers to express the claims that indicate the functions test scores are intended to play. Such claims state that (1) the test scores are useful for certain decisions and (2) their use results in overall positive consequences for test users and for society. Each type of claim can serve in a validity argument as a conclusion for its respective inference of "utilization" and "consequence implication." This chapter begins with a justification for starting with uses and consequences when developing and appraising validity arguments. It describes how the functional roles of the three tests introduced in the previous chapter are presented to the public. The publicly available communication about the tests does not use the technical language of argument-based validity, but this chapter shows how some of the intended score uses and their consequences can be stated in an argument-based validity framework.

Why Start With Use and Consequences?

The *Standards*'s definition of validity as "the degree to which evidence and theory support the interpretations of test scores for proposed uses of test scores" (AERA et al., 2014, p. 1) gives test use a central role in validation. This positioning of test use as central is a logical outcome from a historical evolution. Cureton (1951) was concerned that testers provide solid advice about validity for particular uses. Cronbach (1971) included "usefulness for decision making" as one path to pursue for validity inquiry, which Messick (1989) also incorporated into this validity framework as utility and relevance of test scores as well as the social consequences of their use. Nuances of variation in the role of test uses and consequences for validation are recognized (Kane, 2013; Shepard, 1993, 1997), but overall, the statement in the *Standards*—that validity refers to the interpretations of test scores for proposed uses—captures the mainstream view, which has been embraced with the expression "assessment use argument" even replacing "validity argument" for some researchers (Bachman & Palmer, 2010; Mislevy, 2018).

The consequences of test score use are considered the final conclusion of a validity argument because "tests are commonly administered in the expectation that some benefit will be realized from the interpretation and use of the scores intended by the test developers" (AERA et al., 2014, p. 19). A claim about consequences serving as the conclusion for a validity argument reflects the influence of Messick (1989). In his view, "the functional worth of testing depends not only on the degree to which the intended purposes are served but also on the consequences of the outcomes produced" (p. 85). Accordingly, the *Standards* identifies the consequences of testing as one source of evidence in validation research. Explicating the importance of consequences, Kane (2016) noted the sociopolitical context of the United States, where test consequences are part of the public discussion of testing:

Once the courts started to rule on the acceptability of testing programs based on evaluations of differential impact (or "adverse impact") and the potential for racial and ethnic bias, the sponsors of testing programs were forced to attend to this kind of consequence. The ensuing legal and methodological debates centered on questions of validity. (p. 204)

Further, he noted the relevance of cost–benefit analysis for weighing evidence of positive consequences of testing against any negative consequences (Kane, 2013). Such negative consequences need to be considered for the group of intended test takers as a whole as well as for identifiable subgroups. In argument-based validity, the process of cost–benefit analysis is facilitated when testers have explicitly stated the claims about intended test score use and consequences.

Inferences About Use and Consequences

Consequences are shown as the final conclusion for the consequence implication inference in the argument illustrated in Figure 3.1. The two types of warrants supporting the inference, benefits to users and benefits to society, reflect two general types of intended consequences identified in the *Standards*. The first is about the direct benefits that are intended by the test developer and users. Examples of the beneficiaries for such consequences are students who are appropriately placed in classes or guided into courses of study, teachers who obtain information relevant for planning their teaching, employers who are able to make good hiring decisions, and prospective employees who are able to demonstrate their talents to achieve entry and advancement. When consequences refer to the learning that assessment is intended to achieve, support for the inference can ideally come, in part, from examination of both learning processes and outcomes (DiBello, Pellegrino, Gane, & Goldman, 2017). The second type of consequence extends beyond these immediate beneficiaries to impact society in terms of knowledge in the field, accepted practices in education, hiring, and other gatekeeping activities, as well as satisfaction with clinical diagnosis and counseling.

Figure 3.1 also shows the utilization inference, which leads to the claim about the usefulness of the test. The utilization inference typically requires support for at least two types of warrants, one about the utility of the test for its purpose and the other about the decisions to be made based on test scores. Test developers are in the position to express warrants about utility because, as Sireci (2016) put it, no one intends to develop a useless test; tests are developed for a purpose, and it is incumbent on the test developer to state the proposed utility of the test. The decision warrant typically needs to be stated by the test user, who has engaged in a standard-setting process to determine the action to be taken on the basis of certain test scores (Hambleton & Pitoniak, 2006). Such local decision making, guided by information provided by the publisher, should result in decision rules that serve as warrants for the utilization inference. For decision-oriented

Figure 3.1 Schematic Diagram of the Structure of Utilization and Consequence Implication Inferences and Their Claims and Warrants in a Validity Argument

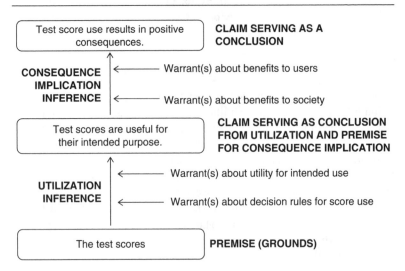

warrants, the assumptions are about the success of the decision rule for achieving the intended results in the context in which the test is used. Accordingly, the backing for each assumption should provide rationales and findings that support the corresponding assumption. Backing for assumptions about utility can come from case studies of test use. For assumptions about decisions, "the backing should make the case for the decision rule" (Kane, 2004, p. 161). A strong case describes a credible standard-setting process, but the process does not deliver "truths" because "just about every aspect of standard setting is a value-laden activity that is subject to disagreement" (Brennan, 1998, p. 9).

Each of the three tests introduced in the previous chapter was created for a particular purpose and with the intent of producing positive consequences. The three differ in their intended uses and consequences as well as in how they are presented to the public. Nevertheless, the publicly available materials about each test provide sufficient information to discern at least some of the warrants and assumptions in their respective validity arguments.

Iowa Assessments: Warrants for Consequence Implication and Utilization

The *Research and Development Guide* for the Iowa Assessments begins with a statement that the intended consequence of test use is "to improve instruction and student learning in kindergarten through twelfth grade in the United States" (University of Iowa, 2015, p. 3). Intended for prospective test users, the *Research and Development Guide* presents the test development rationales and practices as well as the research that has supported test use over the past 85 years. The information, which is available on the Internet, is judicious in its use of technical language from argument-based validity. The presentation nevertheless adheres to the principles of the *Standards* by foregrounding the consequences and uses of the Iowa Assessments and recognizing the role of the test developer in achieving positive consequences.

Consequence Implication

The intended consequence of the Iowa Assessments is summarized in Table 3.1, which states the claim that serves as the conclusion for the consequence implication inference as well as its two supporting warrants and their respective assumptions. Warrant 1 refers to how the positive consequence of improving instruction and learning is to be achieved through a range of uses of the test results, including growth monitoring and comparison with standards to make instructional decisions. The assumptions

Table 3.1   Claim, Warrants, and Assumptions for the Consequence Implication Inference in the Validity Argument for the Iowa Assessments

Claim: The use of the Iowa Assessments improves instruction and learning for students in Kindergarten through Grade 12 in the United States.

User Benefit Warrant and Assumptions	*Social Benefit Warrant and Assumptions*
Warrant 1: Students' learning is improved through the use of systematic monitoring of their growth in core content areas and comparison with known standards to make instructional decisions, including teaching strategies, placement, and selection for targeted interventions.	Warrant 2: Test results can be used "to understand the process of social change through education" (University of Iowa, 2015, p. 149).
A.1.1 The test development process is explained to scores users in sufficient detail to enable them to discern the relevance of the test to their curriculum and needs.	A.2.1 Tests are given systematically over time.
A.1.2 Recommendations are provided for appropriate test uses.	A.2.2 Test results are disaggregated to reveal trends for particular demographics.
A.1.3 Guidelines for reporting score results are provided to maximize the probability that they will be interpreted appropriately.	

identify what the test developer assumes is needed for Warrant 1 to be credible. The three assumptions—one about information on the test development process, a second with recommendations for appropriate test uses, and a third providing guidelines for reporting score results—identify what is necessary to achieve the positive consequences. The support, or backing, for these assumptions appears in the *Research and Development Guide,* which acknowledges the test developer's responsibility for promoting positive consequences from test score use and provides the information expected to be necessary for doing so.

Warrant 2 states a social benefit that is relevant to the claim that the Iowa Assessments improve instruction and learning for students. The warrant states that the test results can be used to understand the process of social change through education. The systematic data collection over time presents a longitudinal picture of change in student learning associated with changing demographics, curricula, or policy. The assumptions therefore state that the tests should be given systematically over time, in order to collect sufficient longitudinal data to document changes, and that results are disaggregated to reveal trends for particular demographics. The backing for these assumptions is also in the *Research and Development Guide,* where disaggregated longitudinal results are presented and interpreted to reveal social change.

Utilization Inference

The utilization inference leads to the claim that the Iowa Assessments are useful for "a variety of important educational purposes that involve the collection and use of information describing either an individual student or groups of students" (University of Iowa, 2015, p. 3). Two types of warrants are used for supporting the utilization inference. One states the intended uses for the test, and the other states the actual decision rules applied to the test scores. The *Research and Development Guide* states 10 examples of intended uses for the Iowa Assessments scores, which are shown as warrants in Table 3.2. Research required for supporting these warrants addresses certain assumptions, which are not given in the table due to their number. For example, Warrant 7 stating that scores can be used for comparing student performance across groups is based on assumptions about the norming research. Accordingly, the *Guide* (pp. 11–20) states the assumptions that were taken into account when the sampling procedures were undertaken for the 2010 and 2011 norming studies. For Warrant 3 about monitoring growth by describing change in student performance over time, several assumptions are stated. They include that the domain model for the test is based on a learning continuum or progression that encompasses development over the 12 years of schooling, that a relevant statistical growth model is used to describe and predict growth over time, that field testing demonstrated the test results reflected expected growth trajectories, and that the results are interpretable by the teachers and others who will use them. The rationales and studies for these assumptions are provided.

The second type of warrant, the decision rule, is exemplified by Warrants 11 and 12 in Table 3.2. Warrant 11 illustrates a hypothetical decision rule for using test scores to identify students at risk, the use stated by Warrant 5. The assumptions underlying Warrant 11 would call for evidence showing that the decision rule identifies the students who can benefit from the individualized instruction and that it does not neglect others who would also benefit. Warrant 12 illustrates a hypothetical decision rule to be applied to groups for making comparisons as stated by Warrant 7. One assumption underlying Warrant 12 would be that grade-level standards are appropriate for the decision context because of similarities between the sample used for norming and the class in which the decision rule is applied. A second assumption would be that school expectations are for students to perform

Table 3.2 Claim, Warrants, and Assumptions for the Utilization Inference in the Validity Argument for the Iowa Assessments

Claim: Iowa Assessments are useful for "a variety of important educational purposes that involve the collection and use of information describing either an individual student or groups of students" (University of Iowa, 2015, p. 3).

Utility Warrants	Decision Warrants[1]
Warrant 1: To identify strengths and weaknesses in student performance—Make relative comparisons of student performance from one content area to another.	Warrant 11: Students scoring two standard deviations below the class mean should be offered individual help sessions.
Warrant 2: To inform instruction—Make judgments about past and future instructional strategies.	A.11.1 Students with scores lower than this score level will benefit from the individual help provided.
Warrant 3: To monitor growth—Describe change in student performance over time.	
Warrant 4: To measure performance in terms of core standards—Determine the degree to which students have acquired the essential skills and concepts of core standards.	A.11.2 Students with scores higher than this score level will succeed without any individual help.
Warrant 5: To implement Response to Intervention (RTI)—Identify students at risk for poor learning outcomes who may benefit from intensive, systematic learning interventions.	
Warrant 6: To inform placement decisions—Place students into programs; assign students to different levels of a learning program.	Warrant 12: Mean class scores below the grade-level standards indicate areas of weakness should be investigated and instruction should be redesigned.
Warrant 7: To make comparisons—Compare student performance with that of local, state, and national groups.	
Warrant 8: To evaluate programs—Provide information that can be used to evaluate the effectiveness of curricular changes.	A.12.1 School conditions are in place for classes to achieve above grade-level standards.
Warrant 9: To predict future performance—Use current information to predict future student performance.	
Warrant 10: To support accountability—Provide reliable and valid information that can be used to meet district and state reporting requirements. (University of Iowa, 2015, pp. 3–4)	

[1] Warrants 11 and 12, with their respective assumptions, illustrate the types that could be developed by test users to serve as decision rules to work toward goals set in their own school.

above national norms in mathematics. These types of assumptions would require support by locally conducted inquiry investigating the values, practices, and learning experiences of participants in the schools. Overall, the Iowa Assessments provide some good examples of how a program of research engaged with a well-defined pool of prospective users can provide information directly applicable to test score use across a range of contexts.

TOEFL iBT: Warrants for Consequence Implication and Utilization

The consequence implication and utilization inferences for the TOEFL iBT lead to the claims that "the test results are used appropriately and have positive consequences" and that the test is useful for aiding "in admissions and placement decisions at English-medium institutions of higher education and to support English-language instruction" (Educational Testing Service, 2011a, p. 3). These claims appear in Volume 4 of the *TOEFL iBT^TM Research Insight*, Series 1, a volume in a publicly available set of reports intended for score users. Like the user guide for Iowa Assessments, these reports do not use the language of argument-based validity, but the warrants and assumptions intended to support claims about consequences and use are evident.

Consequence Implication

The first part of the claim about consequences refers to the positive effects that can ensue from appropriate use of test results. The warrant provides more detail with the statement that use of test scores results in decisions that increase the probability of success for admitted students. The users who benefit from such decisions are the universities that count on English-language use to operate as intended as well as individual teachers and students, both of whom are negatively affected if students do not have the basic competencies required to participate in instruction. These positive benefits can be expected only if the admissions process is carried out effectively, and therefore the assumption is that the joint responsibility for test score use rests with both the test publisher and university personnel. Some support, or backing, for this assumption comes from the test documentation provided by the publisher, but additional backing would need to come from studies in the field of actual observed and reported benefits.

Warrant 2 for the utilization inference is about the broader effects of the use of TOEFL iBT scores. This warrant states the intent for the TOEFL iBT to promote positive learning processes to leverage the fact that teachers and

Table 3.3   Claim, Warrants, and Assumptions for the Consequence Implication Inference in the Validity Argument for the TOEFL iBT

Claim: "The test results are used appropriately and have positive consequences" (Educational Testing Service, 2011a, p. 3).

User Benefit Warrant	*Social Benefit Warrant*
Warrant 1: Students with adequate English-language proficiency to succeed are granted admission to the university, and those without the necessary English-language proficiency are not admitted. A.1.1 There is a joint responsibility between the test publisher and university personnel responsible for effective admissions decisions.	Warrant 2: The inclusion of test tasks simulating the cognitive complexity and academic language of academic tasks on the TOEFL iBT will "prompt the creation and use of test preparation materials and activities that would more closely resemble communicatively oriented pedagogy in academic English courses" (Educational Testing Service, 2011a, p. 9). A.2.1 Innovations from the test, including academic speaking tasks and tasks requiring integration such as the combination of reading and writing for task completion, will appear in course materials and teaching. A.2.2 In addition to providing example test tasks to materials developers, materials explaining the relationship between communicative English teaching and the TOEFL iBT test design will be instrumental in creating changes in teaching. A.2.3 Research on English-language classes internationally shows changes in teaching and materials over time.

learners direct their efforts in their language study to success on this high-stakes test. The assumptions underlying this warrant are that effects of the test design will appear in course materials and teaching, that materials explaining the connection between test task design and communicative language teaching will be instrumental in effecting change, and that longitudinal research on English-language classes internationally will show changes in teaching and materials. The first two assumptions are supported by the documentation about the test itself and the materials made available to professionals in English-language teaching (Educational Testing Service, 2012). The latter assumption has been supported, to some degree, by Wall and Horák's (2006) qualitative study of changes in English-language teaching in one setting. Research is needed to provide additional backing.

Utilization

The utilization inference leading to the claim that the test is useful for aiding in admissions and placement decisions and for influencing English-language instruction requires support for two types of warrants. As shown in Table 3.4, Warrant 1 states the utility of the test for making decisions about admissions and placement for nonnative speakers of English. One assumption underlying the utility warrant is that the test scores are judged to be useful in English-medium higher education. The widespread use of generations of the TOEFL in North America over the past 60 years (Taylor & Angelis, 2008) might serve as one source of evidence for this assumption, but research about the claim of utility ideally would be supported by data about test use and perceptions about utility internationally. Such data should be presented at least internally to maintain a rationale for specific test uses, but such research can also be of interest to the field (e.g., Kokhan, 2012). Other assumptions underlying this warrant are that descriptive information provided to score users helps them to interpret test scores appropriately, guidance provided by the publisher is used by institutions for setting their own admissions standards for TOEFL iBT scores (Educational Testing Service, 2005), and empirical research provides evidence about the effectiveness of test score use. All three assumptions require backing from the study of test score use in the field. For example, a study targeting the fourth assumption examined the effectiveness of speaking scores in making decisions at universities in the United States about international teaching assistants, one subpopulation for whom admissions and placement decisions are made (Xi, 2008). Such research has shown the inadequacy of single-correlation coefficients between test scores and a criterion measure. Instead, a careful examination of the test score profiles, taking into account subpopulation characteristics, is more revealing (e.g., Ginther & Yan, 2017).

The two decision warrants provided in Table 3.4 state the admissions and placement decisions made based on test scores at Iowa State University, as displayed on the webpage with information for international applicants. The publisher does not set cut scores for university admissions, but it provides materials for conducting workshops that enable faculty to understand the scores and come to an agreement about the appropriate cut scores for their institutions. The assumptions, which focus on test score use at a single institution, are stated in a way that would allow for evidence to be gathered to investigate the credibility of the assumptions, as Kokhan (2012) did at the University of Illinois at Urbana-Champaign. Such investigations should at least be written as internal technical reports documenting the rationale for the cut scores on the basis of locally conducted inquiries to assess benefits to users and the adequacy of support for helping admitted students to succeed (Ginther & Yan, 2018).

Table 3.4 Claim, Warrants, and Assumptions for the Utilization Inference in the Validity Argument for the TOEFL iBT

Claim: The TOEFL iBT is useful to aid "in admissions and placement decisions at English-medium institutions of higher education and to support English-language instruction" (Educational Testing Service, 2011a, p. 3).

Utility Warrant	Decision Warrants[1]
Warrant 1: The test scores are useful for making decisions about admissions and placement for nonnative speaker of English applicants to English-medium educational institutions.	Warrant 2: A total TOEFL iBT score of 71 or higher in addition to scores of at least 17 in both the Writing and Speaking sections meet the English proficiency requirement for undergraduate admissions to Iowa State University.
A.1.1 Test users judge the scores to be useful for their purposes in English-medium higher education.	A.2.1 The decision rule results in admitted students whose academic English performance is sufficient for their success in university courses.
A.1.2 Descriptive information provided to score users helps them to interpret test scores appropriately.	A.2.2 The admitted students are at an appropriate level to benefit from additional placement testing that identifies the best course placement in ESL instruction.
	A.2.3 The university offers courses that serve the English-language needs of admitted students.
A.1.3 Guidance provided by the publisher is used by institutions for setting their own admissions standards for TOEFL iBT scores.	Warrant 3: Test takers with a TOEFL iBT total score of 100 or higher are exempt from additional English placement testing.
A.1.4 Empirical research provides evidence about the effectiveness of test score use.	A.3.1 The decision rule results in exempted students succeeding in academic English performance without additional instruction.
	A.3.2 The students who are not exempted are likely to be placed in an academic writing and/or speaking class, based on additional placement testing.
	A.3.3 The university offers academic writing courses that serve the English-language needs of students placed in the courses.

[1] Warrants 2 and 3 are examples of the types of warrants that can be stated and justified by a test user. These were the actual decision rules used by Iowa State University in 2018, as stated in the published information for international applicants.

MSCEIT: Warrants for Consequence Implication and Utilization

The MSCEIT was developed for psychology research investigating facets of human intelligence, and although research continues, the test is now marketed by Multi-Health Systems (MHS) of Toronto. The publisher offers just a sketch of the test and its use in publicly available documents, but makes more thorough user manuals available to qualified buyers. In the public flyer, the MSCEIT is advertised as "suitable for all manner of corporate, educational, research, and therapeutic settings" (MHS Assessments, n.d., p. 1), a claim that would require a large number of warrants and assumptions, but exactly what these would be is not detectable. The research articles also make reference to potential educational and social uses of the MSCEIT in addition to its use for investigating intelligence, which the authors claim is a positive consequence of test use. The example claims, warrants, and assumptions presented here were discerned from the reports of research, so they provide examples of how uses and consequences can be stated for research uses of a test.

Warrants and Assumptions About Consequence Implication

The overall claim about the positive consequences of the MSCEIT is that it plays a role in understanding human intelligence. The authors argue, "there has been much to gain and little to lose from working out the reasoning employed to understand emotions" (Mayer et al., 2016, p. 298). It is not obvious from the reports of research what the particular user benefits would be, but a warrant about the social benefit of the MSCEIT research program might be stated as follows:

Warrant 1: Development and use of the MSCEIT plays a critical role in advancing the scientific study of diverse aspects of human abilities.

Published papers summarizing research on the MSCEIT identify the assumptions underlying Warrant 1. One is that "educators can develop new curricula that explicitly focus on the units of problem solving and that explain the varieties of reasoning involved; educators who understand the units and operators involved may better teach problem solving in the area" (Mayer et al., 2016, p. 297). A second assumption is that knowledge gained from research on the MSCEIT "enables computer scientists to create expert systems that emulate human reasoning—matters of importance with the growing relevance of expert computer systems in our lives" (Mayer et al., 2016). A third assumption is that awareness of individual variation in emotional intelligence in society can benefit interpersonal relationships and even "make that quality more prized and sought after by those who do not possess the same degree of ability" (Allen, Sylask, & Mayer, 2016, p. 5). Support is not provided for these assumptions, but it would be possible to investigate the extent to which support could be found.

Warrant and Assumptions About Utilization

The developers of the MSCEIT claim that the test is useful for scientific inquiry into human intelligence (Mayer et al., 2016). There are undoubtedly some decisions that are made on the basis of test results during the course of the research, but it is not clear what these are, so hypothetical decision warrants are not suggested here. In contrast, the utility warrant for this claim is easy to discern:

Warrant 1: The test is useful for defining and investigating the construct of emotional intelligence.

One assumption is that research on the development of the MSCEIT is instrumental in defining the construct of emotional intelligence. The test developers' own experience with the test is relevant as backing: "Our understanding of emotional intelligence has depended on the development of ability measures" (Mayer et al., 2016, p. 298). Other backing could come from detailed documentation of this line of intelligence research showing the precise roles that the measure has played. A second assumption asserts the uniqueness of the emotional intelligence construct: The MSCEIT can predict outcomes beyond those predicted by other measures of emotion, intelligence, and other recognized constructs. The test developers stated this assumption as follows: "Ultimately, the value of the MSCEIT as a measure of EI will be settled by studies of its validity and utility in predicting important outcomes over and above conventionally measured emotion, intelligence, and related constructs" (Mayer, Salovey, Caruso, & Sitarenios, 2003, p. 104). A third assumption is that results from research using the MSCEIT are interpretable within a program of research investigating the structure of intelligence. Backing for this assumption would need to come from a demonstration of the utility of the emotional intelligence construct in the mainstream intelligence research.

Potential Rebuttals

Rebuttals for utilization and consequence implication limit or refute the credibility of claims about intended uses and positive consequences.

Rebuttals can refer to the entire scope of the claim, or they can refer to certain individuals or groups for whom the validity argument would not adequately support the stated uses and consequences. For the Iowa Assessments, for example, the claim for the consequence implication is that test use improves instruction and student learning in schools in the United States. A rebuttal for the consequence implication inference would be the following:

> Teachers target achieving mean test scores above those of the norm group as the primary goal of instruction.

The Iowa Assessments are intended to assess students' achievement in important areas of the curriculum but not in all that they learn in school, as explained in the *Research and Development Guide*. Therefore, negative consequences of using the Iowa Assessments would result if what is tested were to become the central focus for teaching. This rebuttal is stated as universally relevant, but one could also state a rebuttal pertaining to students whose life and schooling experience has been exclusively in urban areas or in another culture:

> Unfamiliar test content drawn from scenarios in rural America creates anxiety and distrust in students in urban schools for whom the test seems to contain unfamiliar content.

The positive consequence claimed for the TOEFL includes a positive effect on English-language teaching around the world. The design of the test is intended to prompt the creation and use of test preparation materials and activities that would more closely resemble communicatively oriented pedagogy in academic English courses. A rebuttal would be the following:

> In many settings, teachers do not have control over the curriculum and materials, and those who make decisions are unaware of the design of the TOEFL.

In settings where these conditions were found to hold, the rebuttal would be supported, limiting the scope of the positive consequences.

The positive consequence claimed for the MSCEIT is that it plays a role in understanding human intelligence, which affects the value placed on this attribute in society. A rebuttal would be the following:

> In work settings using the MSCEIT, some candidates are unable to compete for positions due to their low MSCEIT scores, even if they have important job skills in other areas.

Where the MSCEIT scores are emphasized above all else, resulting in loss of some applicants, the utilization inference would not be plausible. These rebuttals depict examples in which certain conditions result in limits on achieving the intended consequences for certain identifiable subgroups of test takers. When rebuttals are not supported by evidence, they may remain as concerns for test users, but they cannot be considered to limit or refute the validity argument. The rebuttals also illustrate why some testers argue that the consequences of testing should not be considered part of a validity argument. Consequences extend beyond the control of a test developer; they rest on the actions, circumstances, and values of others out in the world. However, because test score use and consequences are normally the reasons for testing, it is difficult to comprehend how they could be irrelevant to evaluating validity of test use. The *Standards* states the need to support claims made about positive consequences. However, the *Standards* stops short of recognizing all negative consequences of testing as relevant to a validity argument. Intended consequence implications stem from the grounds that the test is useful for its purpose. When a test is misused, the utilization inference cannot be warranted, no conclusion about utility can be drawn, and therefore no grounds are developed for a consequence implication.

Finally, despite the demonstrated validity of certain test interpretations and uses, test use may have certain unintended negative consequences, such as making test takers unhappy about the time and cost of test taking, making teachers frustrated by the disproportionate amount of attention students give to test preparation, or making employers annoyed by the weight given to the test scores relative to other aspects of candidates' profiles. Such unintended consequences of testing may or may not be relevant to the validity argument, depending on the warrants that are stated in support of consequence implications.

Conclusion

The examples in this chapter demonstrate the fundamental role of uses and consequences of testing that the *Standards* indicate should serve as a starting point for validation. Nevertheless, controversy remains in the field, with some testers arguing that validation should encompass only the substantive and consistency aspects of score meaning (Borsboom, 2006; Cizek, 2012; Lissitz & Samuelsen, 2007; Popham, 1997). In fact, argument-based validity accommodates this perspective with its contingent approach:

> Under the argument-based approach to validation, it is legitimate to focus on an interpretation to the exclusion of any uses, but it is not legitimate to evaluate only the interpretation and then to claim that one has validated a testing [program] as a whole, including a proposed interpretation and proposed uses. (Kane, 2016, p. 207)

Perhaps the most compelling reason for including test uses and consequences is that these functional roles of the test are important for the way other aspects of the validity argument are developed. In this sense, one might add to Sireci's (2016) question, "Why would we develop tests that we expect will never be used for a practical purpose?" a second question: How could we develop tests without first defining their intended uses and consequences? The topics in the following chapters—how the construct is defined, how reliability is conceived, and how the test content is developed—all hinge on the intended test uses and consequences.

Chapter 4

CONSTRUCT-RELATED INFERENCES: EXPLANATION AND EXTRAPOLATION

This chapter explains the claims and inferences that are used to express the substantive meaning of test scores as constructs. "The term *construct* is used in the *Standards* to refer to the concept or characteristic that a test is designed to measure" (AERA et al., 2014, p. 11). According to the *Standards,* examples of constructs are "mathematics achievement, general cognitive ability, racial identity attitudes, depression, and self-esteem" (p. 11). These examples include one of the constructs assessed by the Iowa Assessments: mathematics achievement. The construct assessed by the MSCEIT is not general cognitive ability but the specific cognitive ability of emotional intelligence. The construct assessed by the TOEFL iBT is academic English proficiency. The names of tests may indicate the intended substantive meaning of test scores, but test names are not sufficiently technical for guiding validation research. This chapter looks at how the constructs that underlie score interpretation can be specified and investigated in argument-based validation through the use of explanation and extrapolation inferences.

Constructs in Validity Arguments

Argument-based validity departs from the historical thread outlined in Chapter 1 of placing constructs ever-more central to the process of validation. The construct-centric perspective, however, persists in the 2014 *Standards.* According to the *Standards*, the construct interpretation should serve as the "conceptual framework" for the test, and it is the conceptual framework that "points to the kinds of evidence that might be collected to evaluate the proposed interpretation in light of the purposes of testing" (AERA et al., 2014, pp. 1–2). In contrast, Kane saw the exclusive reliance on the construct for developing a program of validation as problematic, in part because of the vagueness of most construct theories. Whereas some psychologists have rigorous parameters that their constructs must adhere to, Shepard (1993) noted, "the notion that constructs refer [only] to hidden psychological traits has been abandoned" (p. 413). This is perhaps the type of statement that prompted Slaney's (2017) analysis, which found that "the concept 'construct' has fallen prey to a fair degree of conceptual carelessness" (p. 210). Moreover, the goal of using a construct as the basis for a conceptual framework proved to be unrealistic for at least one testing program (Chapelle, Enright, & Jamieson, 2010). Whether the liberalization of the term *construct* is seen as deliberate or negligent, the implication is that testers need to understand what, if any, role constructs play in validity arguments.

Argument-based validity addresses the fact that constructs are typically insufficient as the sole basis for guiding validation. In argument-based validity, a construct framework is replaced by an interpretation/use argument framework. Within an interpretation/use argument, if a construct is important for expressing the substantive meaning of the test scores, the construct must be specified. Such a specification, however, can be made from the standpoint of the liberal view of constructs following from Cronbach (1971) and Messick (1989), who defined constructs as a means for naming meaningful categories from disparate parts. Messick outlined two types of meanings that such categories can have:

> Test behaviors are often viewed as samples of domain behaviors (or essentially similar to domain behaviors) for which predictions are to be made or inferences drawn. Test behaviors are also viewed as signs of other behaviors that they do not ordinarily resemble and as indicants of underlying processes or traits. (p. 15)

In other words, constructs can legitimately have different types of meanings. Rather than prescribing what constructs must be, argument-based validity takes into account the importance of the different possible meanings for various test scores by providing testers with the tools to define the inferences in the validity argument in a manner that expresses the intended substantive meanings of the construct.

Explanation Inferences for Traits

Messick (1989) defined a trait as "a relatively stable characteristic of a person—an attribute, enduring process, or disposition—which is consistently manifested to some degree when relevant, despite considerable variation in the range of settings and circumstances" (p. 15). In other words, the substantive meaning of a trait-type construct is expressed as human capacities rather than what the construct does (performance) and where it is displayed (types of tasks or contexts). An operational definition specifies the conditions under which relevant performance is observed, as explained by Cronbach (1971). However, from a trait perspective, the operational definition is an instrument for obtaining consistent samples of performance that allows testers to make an inference about the test takers' characteristics

Figure 4.1   Schematic Diagram of the Structure of the Explanation
Inference With Its Claim and Warrants to Serve as Part of a
Validity Argument

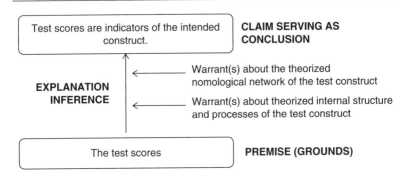

rather than a definition of contexts required for expressing the substantive
sense of the construct.

Trait-type constructs can be hypothesized to be real (i.e., existing to
varying degrees in all humans), or they can be, as the term *construct* suggests, constructed by researchers who find them useful for explaining performance consistencies. The argument-based validity approach is neutral as
to the reality of traits, but if the substantive sense of the score is based on
a trait-type construct, the validity argument includes an explanation inference leading to a claim about the construct, as illustrated in Figure 4.1.
Kane (1992) called this a theory-based inference "involving possible explanations or connections to other constructs" (p. 530). The two main types of
warrants that can support the theory-based, or explanation, inference in a
validity argument are based on two ways of defining traits.

Warrants for Explanation

Warrants for explanation are illustrated for the MSCEIT because emotional intelligence is an example of a trait-type construct: It is defined as
abilities that affect performance across a range of contexts. In the validity
argument for the MSCEIT, the explanation inference leads to the claim that
scores reflect the ability to recognize and reason about emotions. The warrants provide more specific statements about how the construct is defined:
a nomological theory, which states the substantive sense of the construct
relative to other constructs, as Cronbach and Meehl (1955) explained, and
the internal structure of components of the construct, which can include a
process model, as introduced by Embretson (1983). Table 4.1 shows how
the two types of warrants, each with its assumptions, are stated.

Table 4.1 Summary of Claim, Warrants, and Assumptions for the Explanation Inference for the MSCEIT

Claim: The scores reflect the ability to recognize and reason about emotions.

Nomological Network Warrant	*Construct Representation Warrant*
Warrant 1: Test scores support the theorized position of emotional intelligence within the nomological network of human abilities and their relationship to certain indicators of workplace success. A 1.1 Correlations between the MSCEIT and tests of crystallized ability and fluid ability are positive but not strong. A 1.2 The items from the MSCEIT and tests of crystallized and fluid ability each load on a different factor in an assessment of overall intelligence. A 1.3 The best model to fit the overall data for the three tests contains the three subconstructs of emotional intelligence, crystallized ability, and fluid ability in addition to the higher-order factor of general intelligence. A 1.4 The scores on the MSCEIT are good predictors of workplace success. A 1.5 The scores on the MSCEIT predict workplace success better than measures of general intelligence do.	Warrant 2: Test scores support the theorized four-component model of emotional intelligence that includes managing emotions to attain specific goals, understanding emotions and emotional language and signals, using emotions to facilitate thinking, and perceiving emotions accurately in oneself and in others (Mayer et al., 2016). A 2.1 Items from all four components of the construct should produce a combined score with high internal consistency and reliability. A 2.2 The items from each of the component scores should produce subscores, each of which has an acceptable internal consistency and reliability. A 2.3 A factor analysis of the item scores for the test should support the theorized correlated four-factor model with a higher-order factor encompassing the four components.

Warrant 1 indicates that the developers of the MSCEIT present emotional intelligence as an ability construct that is "an instance of a standard intelligence that can enrich the discussion of human capacities" (Mayer et al., 2008, p. 503). In other words, the nomological network of emotional intelligence includes other aspects of intelligence in a manner that hypothesizes a relationship between the ability constructs and a lack of relationship between emotional intelligence and personality constructs (Mayer et al., 2016). Their theory also supports hypotheses about the relationship between emotional intelligence and certain indicators of success in workplaces. In keeping with Cronbach and Meehl's (1955) vision of the interplay of construct theory and validation, Mayer, Salovey, and Caruso's research program uses the assumptions to state hypotheses or research questions. Warrant 2 theorizes interrelated components or subconstructs that define the processes entailed in the display of emotional intelligence. Mayer et al. (2016) present the four components as branches of emotional intelligence, which they theorize are "four areas of problem solving necessary to carry out emotional reasoning" (p. 293). Each of the four branches consists of skills and processes, with a theorized progression from basic ones such as identifying or labeling emotions to more complex ones such as discriminating between honest and false representations of emotions. Like the nomological network, this internal representation of the construct provides a basis for formulating assumptions that can be investigated empirically.

Assumptions Underlying Explanation for Trait-Type Constructs

The assumptions underlying Warrant 1 are based on a more detailed nomological network than Warrant 1 provides. Assumptions state specific predictions about the empirical relationships between the MSCEIT and other test and nontest indicators that can be obtained from test takers. Such predictions emanate from the laws of the nomological network, which "may relate (a) observable properties or quantities to each other; or (b) theoretical constructs to observables; or (c) different theoretical constructs to one another" (Cronbach & Meehl, 1955, p. 290). The goal of establishing such laws is that "the investigator who proposes to establish a test as a measure of a construct must specify [its] network or theory sufficiently clearly that others can accept or reject it" (p. 291).

As Mayer et al. (2008) explained, their research program has undertaken to do this for the MSCEIT. Based on the verbal description of the construct theory and research findings, one might sketch the nomological network shown in Figure 4.2. The circles are theorized constructs and the rectangles are observables consisting of scores or other observed indicators. The nomological network encompasses the three types of laws Cronbach and Meehl (1955) outlined: (1) The observable properties of workplace success and scores on the total MSCEIT test are related to each other, as indicated by the double-headed arrow; (2) the construct of emotional intelligence explains the observed scores on the MSCEIT test, as indicated by the single-headed arrow beginning at the construct and terminating at the observed test scores; the construct of emotional intelligence is correlated with observed workplace evaluations, indicated by the double-headed arrow; and (3) emotional intelligence is among the subconstructs that make up general intelligence, as indicated by the single-headed arrow originating in the intelligence construct and terminating at the emotional intelligence construct.

Figure 4.2 Proposed Nomological Network for the Cognitive Construct
of Emotional Intelligence

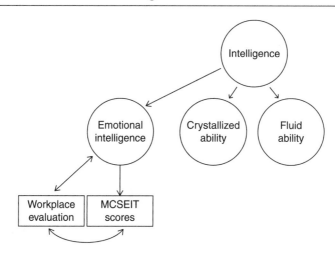

The other two subconstructs of intelligence included in the theory have
been variously named, but one refers to propositional knowledge and verbal ability (crystallized ability) and the other is nonverbal and strategic
abilities (fluid ability; Horn & Cattell, 1966). The nomological network in
Figure 4.2 indicates that emotional intelligence is not strongly related to
these other aspects of general intelligence because no double-headed arrow
connects emotional intelligence to either of them. In sum, the nomological
network shows emotional intelligence as a unique aspect of general intelligence not covered by components of established intelligence theory.

These theorized sets of relationships, or laws, form the basis for assumptions underlying Warrant 1 for the explanation inference. From a theoretical
perspective, some researchers would want to investigate assumptions about
the inclusion of emotional intelligence within the long-established two-
component model and would want to use well-established tests for doing
so. They would specify assumptions, such as Assumptions 1.1 through 1.3,
to be used in stating empirically testable hypotheses. Other researchers with
more applied interests would want to investigate assumptions about the
predictive power of the MSCEIT as an indicator of workplace success
(Assumptions 1.4 and 1.5). The nomological network states that the test
should predict observations of workplace success, which could consist of
multiple different kinds, including both routinely gathered evaluations and
indicators designed specifically for the research. The nomological network
as shown does not specify the type of workplace success, nor does it

attribute any theoretical meaning to the indicators, but such aspects could be added to guide research if assumptions were stated about relationships among different types of workplace success. Research can also be based on what is excluded from the nomological network. The MSCEIT is intended to measure the cognitive construct of emotional intelligence, which is unrelated to psychological factors, according to the construct theory. Psychological factors, therefore, do not appear in the nomological network. Research could investigate the assumption that the MSCEIT is correlated more strongly with the other ability measures in the network than it is with psychological measures of factors such as extroversion and anxiety. In short, the nomological network is a sandbox for construct theory, providing a basis for developing assumptions for warrants about the substantive sense of the construct. Such assumptions form the hypotheses and questions for research whose results are intended to inform the evolution of the construct theory (Mayer et al., 2008). Assumptions about the nomological network can also extend into the subconstructs of emotional intelligence. For example, MacCann, Pearce, and Roberts (2011) investigated the assumption that the component scores for two tests of emotional intelligence and scores from subscores on an intelligence test should result in two correlated higher-order factors, each with its theorized component scores. Their study did not include the MSCEIT, so the results are not directly interpretable with respect to the nomological network developed for the MSCEIT, but the methodology illustrates how tests are used for theory testing in the manner introduced by Cronbach and Meehl (1955) and developed by Campbell and Fiske (1959) with their introduction of the multitrait-multimethod matrix for convergent and discriminant validation designs, based on hypothesized nomological networks. Such theory and research methods are used to investigate what the *Standards* refers to as evidence of relationships with other variables.

Assumptions for Warrant 2 are based on the theoretical properties of the components of the construct of emotional intelligence. Embretson's (1983) methodology for investigating such a construct representation is multicomponent latent trait modeling, which requires test takers' response data on each of the items in addition to raters' scores quantifying the relevant task characteristics. To use Embretson's methodology, the construct representation theory needs to specify how certain characteristics of the test tasks are expected to affect test takers' performance in predictable and quantifiable ways. Elements of this basic idea appear in the process-oriented construct definitions that Kane and Mislevy (2017) refer to as "production system models" and "cognitive diagnosis models." The theorized four-component model of emotional intelligence perhaps does not offer a construct representation that can serve as a basis for specific process-oriented assumptions. Nevertheless, the fact that two of the branches (managing and understanding emotions) of the four-component definition are theorized to be higher level than the other two (using and perceiving emotions) suggests somewhat of a productions system model positing that using and perceiving emotions come prior to the higher-level components. The warrant about the four components requires assumptions that can be empirically tested, as stated in Assumptions 2.1 through 2.3 in Table 4.1. As more is learned about the cognitive construct of emotional intelligence, additional precision may be added to the four-branch construct theory, which may in turn support clearer process-oriented assumptions, opening the door to new validation procedures.

Today, quantitative model testing is seen as only one of many ways of investigating test-taking processes. Response processes, named as one of the five types of validity evidence in the *Standards*, are defined more broadly, in part due to the role of technology in recording test-taking behaviors as well as the use of qualitative methods to gather process data. Two recent volumes provide state-of-the-art accounts of work in this area. Ercikan and Pellegrino (2017) define response processes as the "thought processes, strategies, approaches, and behaviors of examinees when they read, interpret, and formulate solutions to assessment tasks" (p. 2). Similarly, but more broadly, Hubley and Zumbo (2017) define response processes as "the mechanisms that underlie what people do, think, or feel when interacting with, and responding to, the item or task and are responsible for generating observed test score variation" (p. 2). The use of technology to gather data on response processes as well as qualitative methodologies have been illustrated in a number of validation studies over the past 30 years. These serve as examples of the approach and the types of warrants and assumptions that are investigated in such research (Ercikan & Pellegrino, 2017). These examples demonstrate that the use of such methods to investigate warrants underlying the explanation inference requires a process-oriented construct definition stated as assumptions about the expected test-taking processes (Wise, 2017).

Extrapolation Inferences for Performance

Cronbach and Meehl (1955) acknowledged that performance-type constructs play a role "in the early stages of development of a construct or even at more advanced stages when our orientation is thoroughly practical," and that "little or no theory in the usual sense of the word need be involved" (p. 292). For such cases, they introduced extrapolation as follows: "Even though no unobservables or high-order theoretical constructs are introduced, an element of inductive extrapolation appears in the claim that a cluster including some elements not-yet-observed has been identified" (p. 292). Cronbach and Meehl's "theory in the usual sense" was, for Messick (1989), theory in just one sense. For Messick, depending on the intended interpretation and use of test scores, trait theory was not inherently better than response class theory (p. 15), which underlies performance-based construct definition. Accordingly, Kane (2013) provided a means for expressing performance-type constructs, which he referred to as "observable attributes" within a defined domain. He pointed out that "we do not have to wait for full explanations of observed regularities in performance before making use of these regularities (e.g., in the form of observable attributes)" (pp. 33–34).

Kane et al. (1999) used the term *target domain* to refer to "the full range of performances included in the [test score] interpretation" (p. 7).

The target domain should be defined broadly enough to represent the kinds of performances that are of interest to parents, teachers, students, and state legislators (if appropriate), even if this leads to some fuzziness in the boundary of the domain. The point is not that ambiguity is desirable but, rather, that it is not such a serious threat that we should be willing to trivialize the target domain in order to get rid of it. In particular, we want to avoid the trap of severely limiting the target domain in order to make some statistical model applicable. It is more important that the target domain reflect the educational outcomes that are of interest in interpreting assessment scores than it be stated with great precision. (p. 8)

Further, they used *target score* to refer to "the examinee's expected score over all possible performances in the target domain" (p. 7). Unlike Cureton's (1951) criterion series or Cronbach and Meehl's (1955) nomological network, the target domain is defined for the benefit of conveying score meaning to test users, rather than solely for use by researchers seeking criterion measures or a basis for hypothesis testing. Nevertheless, the concept of target domain is productive for research because it is needed to specify the warrants that can support the extrapolation inference, as shown in Figure 4.3.

Warrants for Extrapolation

None of the three example tests has scores interpreted solely on the basis of performance in a defined target domain, but the target domain of academic English use helps to define the substantive sense of the TOEFL iBT

Figure 4.3   Schematic Diagram of the Structure of the Extrapolation Inference With Its Claim and Warrants to Serve as Part of a Validity Argument

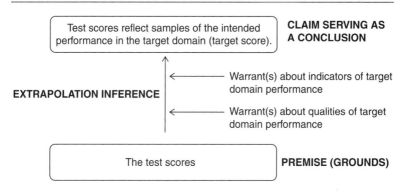

scores. The extrapolation inference in the TOEFL iBT validity argument leads to the claim that scores reflect the academic English performance that is similar to students' performance in an English-medium university, the target domain. Warrants for extrapolation express a comparison between the test performance and the performance in the target domain, as illustrated by the two types of warrants shown in Table 4.2 that support the extrapolation inference for the TOEFL iBT validity argument. Each warrant refers to the target domain of English-medium institutions of higher education, which is large and complex with "some fuzziness in the boundary of the domain," as Kane et al. (1999, p. 8) put it. Each of the warrants suggests a type of analysis that might be used to find relevant evidence, but a clearer picture of the required research comes from the assumptions.

Assumptions Underlying Extrapolation

The first warrant, that academic language performance assessed by the TOEFL iBT tasks accounts for other indicators of linguistic performance in English-medium universities, entails assumptions about what appropriate indicators can be identified and obtained. The theoretical ideal of indicators as "criterion scores based on an especially thorough (and representative) sample of performances from the target domain" (Kane et al., 1999, p. 10) is of little use in practice. Researchers pursuing such extrapolation-oriented research on the TOEFL have identified the challenges, which include the restriction of range inherent in data gathered from students admitted to universities; systematic differences in data associated with particular subgroups of test takers; the degree of indirectness of indicators, construct

Table 4.2 Summary of Claims, Warrants, and Assumptions for the Extrapolation Inference for the TOEFL iBT

Claim: Scores reflect the academic English performance that is similar to students' performance in an English-medium university, the target domain.

Warrant about indicators of performance	Warrant about performance
Warrant 1: The academic language performance assessed by the TOEFL iBT tasks accounts for other indicators of linguistic performance in English-medium universities. A1.1 TOEFL iBT scores should correlate positively with appropriate indicators of linguistic performance at English-medium universities, which include students' academic placement in English-language courses, students' evaluation of their own language performance at the university, teachers' evaluation of students' linguistic performance, and scores on other tests of academic English. A1.2 TOEFL iBT scores should have positive relationships to indicators of successful academic performance at English-medium universities, including students' grades on course assignments and in courses as well as their grade-point averages.	Warrant 2: The academic language performance assessed by the TOEFL iBT tasks is comparable to the quality of linguistic performance on tasks in English-medium institutions of higher education. A2.1 Human ratings of performance features on the test and on important tasks in the target language use domain reveal construct-relevant similarities. A2.2 Automated quantitative analysis of performance features on the test and on important tasks in the target language use domain reveal construct-relevant similarities. A2.3 Qualitative analysis of performance features on the test and on important tasks in the target language use domain reveal construct-relevant similarities.

underrepresentation, and unreliability of criterion indicators; and the fact that language is but one of many factors contributing to academic success (Bridgeman, Cho, & DiPietro, 2016; Cho & Bridgeman, 2012; Ginther & Yan, 2018). These methodological challenges need to be taken into account in designing and interpreting results from research intended to provide evidence pertaining to Assumptions 1.1 and 1.2.

Assumption 1.1 states the many indicators of linguistic performance that would each be expected to correlate positively with the TOEFL iBT scores. Findings of positive correlations between test scores and each of the indicators support the assumption (Chapelle et al., 2008). However, their interpretation had to take into account the factors affecting the indicators, none of which is the idealized criterion score of Kane et al. (1999) or Cureton (1951). The second assumption relies on indicators of overall academic success produced in the target domain, including grades on course assignments and in courses as well as total grade-point average (GPA). The relationship of the TOEFL iBT scores to such indicators needs to be investigated in view of the fact that "there is no one-to-one correspondence between language and academic performance. Language is a crucial factor in learning, but it is only one of many factors" (Cho & Bridgeman, 2012, p. 424). Such factors as motivation and a supportive environment, which affect the predictive power of any gatekeeping test, have to be taken into account in the interpretation of correlations between test scores and measures of success such as GPA. In such circumstances, a positive relationship should be expected but not a strong relationship, and like other indicators from the target domain, GPA is subject to the same issues of restriction of range and limited reliability.

The second warrant—that the academic language performance assessed by the TOEFL iBT tasks is comparable to the quality of linguistic performance on tasks in English-medium institutions of higher education—also refers to performance in the target domain. In contrast to Warrant 1, however, Warrant 2 focuses on the linguistic performance itself rather than indicators of levels of performance as a single score or academic success. Assumptions about Warrant 2, therefore, require evidence from analysis of the responses that test takers produce. For the TOEFL iBT, the writing and speaking sections require linguistic performance from test takers, who are required to write two essays, each one in response to a particular type of prompt, and respond to several recorded prompts orally. Both the written and oral responses are captured in their respective databases and used for scoring in the operational testing program. The databases are then available for additional analysis to examine the language of the responses compared to language used in academic settings.

Three examples illustrate such research in two studies of writing performance and one study of speaking performance. One study investigated the relationship between human ratings of four linguistic aspects of test takers' performance on the writing tasks and ratings of test takers' performance on an essay they had written for an academic writing course (Llosa & Malone, 2018). The analysis considered the strength of the correlations between corresponding ratings for each performance sample. A second study compared responses on the writing test with the language students used in papers they had written for their graduate-level courses. The analysis used three linguistic features as the bases for quantitative comparisons using multivariate analysis of variance (MANOVA), which found a high degree of similarity overall between the two (Riazi, 2016). A third study compared test takers' responses to the speaking prompts in the TOEFL iBT to their oral language in their academic studies by investigating grammatical, discourse, and lexical features. Their qualitative comparisons found both similarities and differences in the two performances, leading to only equivocal support for the assumption (Brooks & Swain, 2014).

These studies provide a glimpse into new ways of addressing the paradox that test performance is claimed to be relevant to particular contexts of performance but such contexts are too complex to supply clear-cut criterion scores to serve in research. Because argument-based validity is a logic for integrating evidence rather than a deterministic machine for generating proofs, it invites innovation and a range of research methods, which presents an opportunity to engage with disciplinary knowledge in relevant fields (Haertel, 2013). It also demands that researchers explain the logic of their analysis procedures and interpretations.

Combining Explanation and Extrapolation for Interactionalist Constructs

Many test score interpretations have elements of both traits and performance. In these cases, the validity argument would include both an explanation and extrapolation inference, as illustrated in Figure 4.4. Some would argue that the theoretical bases of the two types of interpretations are incommensurable (e.g., Norris, 1983). In contrast, Messick (1989) was attuned to the reality of testing practice, where it is not unusual to have constructs defined somewhere on a continuum between the performance and trait extremes. Introducing a third type of interpretation called an interactionalist construct, Messick pointed out, "Many psychologists, of course, adopt intermediate views, attributing some behavioral consistencies to traits, some to situational factors, and some to interactions between them, in various and arguable proportions" (p. 15). An interactionalist construct definition combines the meaning of trait and performance to indicate that a score signifies a certain trait that is responsible for performance in a defined range of domains. Messick's recognition of the middle ground for construct definition comports with the demands of argument-based validity, which requires the tester to express the intended substantive sense of scores. Doing so often requires both traits and performance domains. Figure 4.4 illustrates how such an interactionalist construct can be specified in a validity argument by including both explanation and extrapolation inferences.

Figure 4.4 Schematic Diagram of the Structure of the Explanation and Extrapolation Inferences With Their Respective Claims and Warrants in a Validity Argument

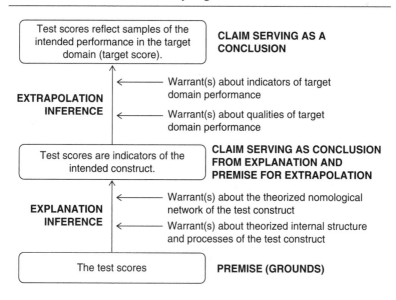

The validity argument for the TOEFL iBT, as presented by Chapelle et al. (2008), contains both explanation and extrapolation inferences. Like many gatekeeping tests, the substantive meaning of the TOEFL iBT scores comes from the consistency in the performance that is attributed to an ability, which may be defined by structures and processes like a trait, as well as to the contexts, situations, or tasks in the target domain. Such interactionalist constructs capture a view pervasive in applied testing that human capacities are best conceived as situated in particular contexts. For example, an assessment of lack of motivation (called "amotivation") for physical education has been developed in the health sciences (Vlachopoulos, Katartzi, & Kontou, 2013). Its validity argument would include an explanation inference with a warrant about the nomological network, including relationships to ability, effort, and variables from self-determination theory (Shen, Wingert, Li, Sun, & Rukavina, 2010). It would also contain an extrapolation inference with warrants about indicators of certain types of physical education tasks or contexts. In this way, the amotivation score meaning is delimited by certain contexts of interest to score users. A second example comes from research investigating the theory and assessment of a model of Internet addiction. The researchers investigated "a nomological network for the Internet addiction components model by testing the predictive accuracy of personality traits on the Internet addiction components factor" (Kuss, Shorter, van Rooij, van de Mheen, & Griffiths, 2014, p. 313). In this way, the network for the trait of addiction was interpreted in connection with contexts of Internet use to express the score meaning as an interactionalist construct.

The tester can choose to include an explanation inference, an extrapolation inference, or both, but "whether test scores are interpretable as signs of trait dispositions or internal states, as samples of domains or response classes, or as some combination, are hypotheses to be validated" (Messick, 1989, p. 15). Such hypotheses need to be stated explicitly with appropriate warrants and assumptions because different theoretical positions "to a large extent, share a common language for speaking of causes, explanations, theoretical terms, theories, and so on—but do not share a common meaning for that language" (Norris, 1983, p. 69). Argument-based validity provides a framework for stating these hypotheses as well as for situating the hypotheses about constructs in their place in the overall validity argument. Such arguments consisting of multiple hypotheses provide a basis for carrying out Cronbach's (1971) vision of the validation process in which "many different techniques are required to examine diverse hypotheses and counterhypotheses. Construct validation requires integration of many studies" (p. 464).

Threats to Construct-Related Inferences

Research conducted to investigate warrants for explanation and extrapolation inferences may yield results supporting or failing to support the intended inferences. Beyond the outcomes of research that fails to find backing for an assumption, testers can also include in the research program rebuttals requiring investigation of the potential limits or threats to the intended inferences. Such limits and threats can apply to the construct interpretation for all test takers or for certain individuals and groups of test takers. Messick (1989) outlined the two general threats to construct validity: construct underrepresentation and construct irrelevant variance. These threats can include bias against certain individuals and subpopulations, for whom the test scores do not have the same construct meaning. Table 4.3 provides examples of the types of rebuttals that could be placed in the respective validity arguments for each of the example tests. Research guided by such rebuttal statements would be designed to reveal the extent to which evidence supported each statement, and under what conditions.

Table 4.3 Examples of Construct-Related Rebuttals That Would Weaken the Explanation or Extrapolation Inference in the Argument for the MSCEIT, TOEFL iBT, and the Mathematics Subtest of the Iowa Assessments

	Source of threat		
Example Test	Construct underrepresentation	Construct irrelevant variance	Bias for or against subpopulations
MSCEIT	The test does not adequately sample from the range of possible scenarios in work settings where emotional intelligence is relevant.	Comprehension of the scenarios in the test requires a high level of English reading ability.	Test takers socialized in a non-Western culture recognize and reason with emotional cues differently.
TOEFL iBT	With only two tasks, the writing section of the test fails to include a sufficient variety of writing relative to the target domain.	In the reading section, the use of primarily selected response items results in the systematic error known as method effects.	Test takers from different language backgrounds perform systematically differently on the test despite having the same level of academic English ability.
Mathematics subtest of the Iowa Assessments	Relative to the core competencies in mathematics, the test assesses only some aspects of mathematics ability.	Test-taking strategies that are not considered part of mathematics ability help students achieve higher scores than they would have based on their mathematics abilities alone.	Students for whom English is not their first language score systematically lower than native speakers of English.

A rebuttal supported by empirical evidence would indicate that the corresponding inference should not be made, and therefore its claim is not plausible, at least in certain cases. Each of these rebuttals represents a potential threat to the construct interpretation made on the basis of test scores. Like the warrants, each one would need to be investigated to determine the degree to which evidence would support the statement. Findings can be used to reject rebuttals, delimit inferences by specifying warrants and claims more narrowly, or undermine the validity argument, depending on the scope of the rebuttal and the findings.

Conclusion

The explanation and extrapolation inferences, each leading to a particular type of construct-related claim, help to make explicit the nature of test constructs, which are formulated and understood in particular communities. Certain communities of research and practice tend to work with particular types of constructs, inferences, warrants, and assumptions. Historically, psychologists tended to concentrate on trait-type constructs and their nomological networks as a basis for explanation. Researchers in education and applied testing, in contrast, typically need to demonstrate the relevance of test scores in a particular context, highlighting extrapolation. Drawing on both perspectives, interactionalist constructs form the basis for many applied tests, like academic English ability, amotivation for physical education, and Internet addiction. Each draws upon a trait construct theory but also delineates a context of relevance for the construct. Some researchers see such interactionalist constructs as an infraction against ontological laws of construct representation because the scores are seen at the same time as signs of traits and samples of performance. Overall, however, most testers working in practice agree that so many test uses exist that a useful validity framework must encompass the potential to include multiple perspectives. Moreover, most testers would align themselves with Cronbach's (1971) goal of seeking usefulness rather than truth in test development and validation.

Alignment with or departure from Cronbach (1971), however, is a matter of researchers' philosophical beliefs and value positions rather than an enduring tenet of validation research. In fact, the utility versus truth divide is one point of exposure for the values that are inherent in defining constructs and conducting validation research. For Messick (1989), values were central to validation, making it necessary for testers to recognize and reveal the value implications of their construct definitions by explaining, for example, the origin of the construct, the rationale for its definition (e.g., why certain perspectives are included and excluded), who benefits and loses when such a construct definition is adopted, and how the construct definition reflects the values of the test users. Such a values analysis requires testers to recognize that certain constructs are not naturally occurring. Instead, each has a social and cultural history, a community where a combination of needs, values, and capabilities yielded certain conceptions of human capacities. When these conceptions, or constructs, are operationalized in tests, they need to be evaluated as part of the context-specific validation process rather than taken to be part of objective structures of human capacities. The use of inferences, warrants, rebuttals, and assumptions in a validity argument is therefore a positive step toward revealing the values inherent in constructs.

Chapter 5

CONSISTENCY-RELATED INFERENCES: GENERALIZATION AND EVALUATION

This chapter presents the inferences in validity arguments that lead to claims about the stability or consistency of the test scores. The range of issues affecting test score consistency are situated under the umbrella of reliability, which the *Standards* presents in a chapter of its own. Despite the separate chapter in the *Standards* as well as the popular notion that validity and reliability are two distinct characteristics of tests, an argument-based validity framework conceives of any claims about reliability of test scores as integral to the validity argument. Testers working in education and research typically recognize the importance of claims about the stability of the test scores, and therefore it is common practice for information for the public to state evidence about reliability. This chapter demonstrates how claims about consistency are expressed in argument-based validity through the use of generalization and evaluation inferences. It illustrates how reliability for each of the three example tests can be expressed in its respective validity argument.

Claims About Score Consistency in Validity Arguments

The significance of reliability for test score interpretation was recognized by Cureton (1951), who defined validity as reliability and relevance. Cronbach also presented reliability as essential by emphasizing that a testing procedure (i.e., the operational definition) had to be specified precisely in order to gather samples of performance that would exhibit consistencies. Reliability is integral to Messick's (1989) definition of a construct as a meaningful interpretation of performance consistency. Because reliability plays an important role in score interpretation, testers need to make and support claims about the degree of error reflected in test scores. Two types of claims capture the main reliability issues, one about the absence of error in the test taking and scoring processes, and the other about the absence of error in the total scores. The estimation of error is the preoccupation of psychometricians, who have theories and technical practices for doing so. Psychometrics is fundamental to test score interpretation and therefore needs to be taken into account in a validity argument. To outline the claims, warrants, and assumptions for argument-based validity, the concept of reliability as the absence of error in test scores in classical test theory will suffice even though other ways of estimating error offer extensions to classical test theory (e.g., Hambleton, Swaminathan, & Rogers, 1991).

Classical test theory relies on the concept of a "true score," which refers to the construct that the observed test score reflects. In other words, for each individual tested, a true score would reflect the level of the capacity tested, but the true score is not observed directly. The observed test score should be thought of as one estimate of the true score. The goal of reliability estimation, broadly speaking, is to gauge the proportion of the observed score that reflects the true score. Doing so requires more than one observed score. Haertel (2006) noted that any set of relevant scores would serve

the purpose of measurement equally well, but they would not all be identical. Taken together, this hypothetical collection of scores represents the general, enduring attribute of interest. Thus, it is important to determine the extent to which any single result of the measurement procedure is likely to depart from the average score over many replications. (p. 65)

Replication is critical to conceptualizing reliability because the degree of error present in test scores becomes evident only when more than one observation is made. As Brennan (2001) put it, testers "can be deceived by having information from only one element of a larger set of interest" (p. 295). The "larger set of interest" refers to the multiple aspects of a construct or types of performances that form the basis of the substantive score meaning. If a tester wants "to get direct information about consistency of performance (i.e., reliability) at least two instances are required. That is, replications in some sense are necessary to estimate reliability" (p. 295). Claims about the absence of error in test scores appear in argument-based validity as the conclusions for two types of inferences: generalization and evaluation.

Generalization Inferences for Test Scores

A generalization inference is made when the test taker's combined scores on the test tasks are accepted as generalizable to performance on all tasks in the assessment domain. The generalization inference treats the observed scores "as if they have been sampled from some universe of observations, involving different occasions, locations, and observers that could have served equally well; in generalizing over conditions of observation, one draws conclusions about the universe of possible observations on the basis of a limited sample of actual observations" (Kane, 1992, p. 529). This means that "it is reasonable to infer that examinees who get a failing score

Figure 5.1   Schematic Structure of the Generalization Inference and Its
Claim and Warrants to Serve as Part of a Validity Argument

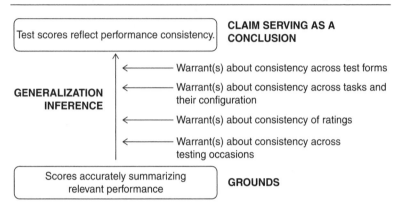

on the sample of [test] tasks would generally perform poorly on the [tasks in the assessment] domain. Examinees with passing scores would be expected to perform adequately, on average, over the assessment domain" (Kane, 1994, p. 152). The assessment domain is not the same as the target domain from Chapter 4, which referred to the contexts beyond the assessment domain in which assessed capacities are intended to be relevant. Instead, the assessment domain refers to the collection of test tasks, testing occasions, and raters who would be expected to produce scores representing the true scores of the test takers. Defining the assessment domain, of course, is a fundamental step in the test development process, which is discussed in the following chapter. Figure 5.1 illustrates the grounds, conclusion, and four types of warrants for a generalization inference in argument-based validity.

Warrants for Generalization

Warrants required to support generalization inferences take into account the four potential sources of error reflected in test scores corresponding to four types of repetitions. One type of error results from inconsistency in the testing materials and procedures from one test form to another. The repeated observations are made using different forms of a test (e.g., Gronlund, 1985). A second type of error can be introduced by inconsistency across test tasks or parts of a test. The repetitions are the multiple test tasks or parts in the test. For example, if the testing procedure includes ambiguous instructions or unknown vocabulary creating misunderstanding by some test takers, the resulting scores would contain error. Moreover, such error sources would be amplified if the sample of performance elicited by the test were too small to capture consistencies (e.g., Cronbach, 1951; Goeman & De Jong, 2018). A third source of error could be introduced due to variations in testing that could occur from one testing occasion to another. The repetition in this case would be the two test administrations occurring at two different times. A fourth source of error would affect score reliability if the processes for rating test takers' responses were inadequately specified, piloted, and controlled. The repetition in this case is the multiple ratings (McNamara, 1996). In short, reliability can refer to several types of consistency, that is, several types of error that can be more or less absent from test scores (Feldt & Brennan, 1989). Therefore, the generalization inference is specified using warrants indicating the types of error to be investigated in the validation research, and the assumptions provide yet another level of detail, which suggests the nature of the investigation.

Assumptions for Generalization

The assumptions underlying generalization warrants can imply or specify such parameters as the number and characteristics of test takers, the technical methods used to estimate reliability, and even an acceptable outcome. The types of reliability reported for the three example tests provide a range of illustrations that are useful for stating assumptions. First, reliability is among the marketing claims made by MHS Assessments for the MSCEIT on the test brochure: "Internal consistency and test-retest analyses were conducted to establish the reliability of the MSCEIT." These two expressions (internal consistency and test-retest) denote two of the four warrants, as shown in Table 5.1. The research reported in several papers by the test developers provides more detail that was interpreted to show the wording for the warrants and their two assumptions. The backing for assumptions underlying Warrant 1 about internal consistency is reported by Mayer, Salovey, and Caruso (2012) as coming from a study with 5,000 test takers. The backing for Warrant 2 is reported by Brackett and Mayer (2003) from a study with 60 participants. The reliabilities stated in the assumptions in Table 5.1 make explicit the levels of consistency the researchers indicate are acceptable in research that serves as backing.

All four warrants about the reliability of scores and their assumptions are addressed in the public document *Reliability and Comparability of TOEFL iBT Scores* (Educational Testing Service, 2011b), which outlines the reliability research on TOEFL iBT. As shown in Table 5.2, Warrant 1 states that the TOEFL iBT scores for each of the four parts (listening, reading, speaking, and writing) and for the total score are consistent across different forms of the test. The assumptions underlying the warrant about consistency across test forms include assumptions about procedures used in test development (Pearlman, 2008), methods of scaling and

Table 5.1 Summary of Claim, Warrants, and Assumptions for the Generalization Inference for the MSCEIT

Claim: The scores on MSCEIT reflect performance consistency.

Warrant About Consistency Across Tasks	*Warrant About Consistency Across Occasions*
Warrant 1: The MSCEIT total scores and each of the four subscores are internally consistent.	Warrant 2: Total test scores are highly consistent across test occasions.
A.1.1 Total score split-half reliability estimates for a large sample of test takers are above .90 if the two halves of the test are constructed to contain equivalent items as specified in the test design.	A.2.1 The test-retest reliability for the total score is at least .80.
A.1.2 Each of the four subscore split-half reliability estimates for a large sample of test takers is above .80 if the two halves of each subtest are constructed to contain equivalent items as specified in the test design.	

equating (Kolen & Brennan, 1995), as well as practices used specifically for the speaking and writing sections, which cannot be equated in the technical sense. The warrant is also supported by an assumption about the consistency of test results across different test forms (Zhang, 2008).

Warrant 2 about internal consistency across test tasks makes assumptions about estimating reliability for the total score in addition to the IRT-based reliabilities (Lord, 1980) for each of the listening and reading sections. It also relies on the assumption that these reliabilities are monitored for each operational test form. Warrant 3 states that the rating consistency of total scores for the writing and speaking sections make them adequate for some purposes. The warrant rests on the assumption that the optimal number of ratings for the acceptable number of tasks was determined by conducting a G-study and D-study (Brennan, 1983), and that the results yielded adequate levels of g-coefficients (Lee & Kantor, 2005). Warrant 4 states that total scores are highly consistent across test occasions, even when different test forms are used, as they are in operational testing. This warrant requires support for the assumptions that scores from test takers who repeat the test show consistency across testing occasions, which has been found (Zhang, 2008). It also relies on the consistency of rating across administrations,

Table 5.2 Summary of Claim, Warrants, and Assumptions for Generalization Inference for the TOEFL iBT

Claim: The scores on TOEFL iBT reflect performance consistency.

Warrant About Consistency Across Forms	Warrant About Consistency Across Tasks	Warrant About Consistency Across Raters	Warrant About Consistency Across Occasions
Warrant 1: TOEFL iBT scores for each of the four parts and for the total score are consistent across different forms of the test.	Warrant 2: Total TOEFL iBT scores have a high degree of internal consistency reliability, and the listening and reading part scores are sufficiently reliable for some purposes.	Warrant 3: The rating consistency of total scores for the writing and speaking sections is adequate for some purposes.	Warrant 4: Total scores are highly consistent across test occasions, even when different forms are used.
A.1.1 Detailed test specifications are used to guide test development.	A.2.1 The average reliability for the total scores is above the .90 advised for high-stakes decision-making.	A.3.1 The optimal number of ratings for the acceptable number of tasks was determined by conducting a G-study and D-study.	A.4.1 Analysis of scores from test takers who repeat the test shows consistency across testing occasions.
A.1.2 Scaling methods are used to maintain comparable scores across test forms.	A.2.2 Average IRT-based reliability estimates for each of the reading and listening sections are adequate.	A.3.2 Average G-coefficient estimates for each of the speaking and writing sections are adequate.	A.4.2 Cross-administration rater consistency in scoring is investigated whenever possible.
A.1.3 Equating methods are used to adjust scores on forms of the reading and listening sections.	A.2.3 Reliability is monitored routinely by calculating a reliability coefficient for each section, for each administration of the test.		A.4.3 The stability of all reliability estimates is monitored for all test administrations.
A.1.4 On the Speaking and Writing sections, correlations with the other sections are monitored.			
A.1.5 Alternate form reliabilities calculated for test takers who chose to take the TOEFL twice within one month are adequate.			

which is stated in the assumption that cross-administration rater consistency in scoring is investigated whenever possible. Assumptions about stability over occasions of testing and rating processes are also investigated by repeatedly checking on other assumptions each time the test is given and the rating is carried out.

The *Guide for the Iowa Assessments* describes the test analysis that supports three types of warrants to authorize the generalization inference for the mathematics achievement test, as shown in Table 5.3. Warrant 1 states that the scores for each subject area of the test at each level are sufficiently consistent across different forms of the test to meet the needs of users and demands of professional standards. The first assumption is that detailed test specifications are used to guide test development to create parallel content across forms. The second assumption is that the test levels 5/6 through 17/18 have been scaled through a Hieronymus scaling process (Petersen, Kolen, & Hoover, 1989) so that scores are interpretable vertically as one continuous test. The third assumption states that the scale is routinely monitored and systematically modified based on test results and curriculum changes, and the fourth assumption states that scores are equated across forms.

Warrant 2 states that scores have a high degree of internal consistency reliability and a sufficiently low standard error of measurement for use in achievement testing and growth monitoring relative to potential competing assessments. The assumptions underlying this warrant for the total mathematics scores are that the median KR-20 and split-half reliability coefficients for the scores at each of the levels has been estimated to be at least .85 in a large national study. A third assumption is that the presentation of standard errors of measurement and conditional standard errors of measurement allow test users to interpret and use scores appropriately. Warrant 3 states that the mathematics scores are sufficiently consistent across test occasions if testing mode is taken into account, and its assumption is that the median test-retest reliability coefficient for the scores on mathematics sections at each of the levels is estimated to be at least .70. The data required to calculate the test-retest reliability came from two administrations of the test to the same group of test takers within an interval of time too short to expect learning to have occurred prior to the second administration. The demonstration of reliability in such a test-retest study is important for a test to be used for the assessment of progress after a period of time in which learning (or other changes) should take place. When test takers' progress is of interest, test users interpret the change in test scores as indicating the degree of change, and they therefore need to interpret the observed change for an individual relative to the degree of error in the scores. One might ideally seek support for another assumption that does not

Table 5.3 Summary of Claim, Warrants, and Assumptions for the Generalization Inference for the Iowa Assessments

Claim: The scores on each subject area test of the Iowa Assessments reflect performance consistency.

Warrant About Consistency Across Forms	*Warrant About Consistency Across Tasks*	*Warrant About Consistency Across Occasions*
Warrant 1: The scores for each subject area of the test at each level are sufficiently consistent across different forms of the test to meet the needs of users and demands of professional standards.	Warrant 2: Scores have a high degree of internal consistency reliability and a sufficiently low Standard Error of Measurement for use in achievement testing and growth monitoring relative to potential competing assessments.	Warrant 3: Scores are sufficiently consistent across test occasions if testing mode is taken into account.
A.1.1 Detailed test specifications are used to create parallel content.	A.2.1 The median KR-20 reliability coefficient for the scores on mathematics sections at each of the levels is estimated to be at least .85 in a large national study.	A.3.1 The median test-retest reliability coefficient for the scores on mathematics sections at each of the levels has been estimated to be at least .70.
A.1.2 The test levels 5/6 through 17/18 have been scaled through a Hieronymus scaling process so that scores are interpretable vertically as one continuous test.	A.2.2 The median split-half reliability coefficients for the scores on the mathematics sections at each of the levels is estimated to be at least .85 in a large national study.	
A.1.3 The scale is routinely monitored and systematically modified based on test results and curriculum changes.	A.2.3 Standard errors of measurement and conditional standard errors of measurement are provided to support test use.	
A.1.4 Scores are equated across forms.		

include the combined error of different occasions of testing and different administration conditions. Demonstrable levels of consistency in test scores are the result of careful planning and execution of detailed test specifications as well as trialing, controlled testing conditions, scoring, and score reporting. As illustrated by the example tests, a range of statistical techniques needs to be applied in order to obtain relevant backing for each of the assumptions underlying the warrants that authorize generalization. In the terms used in the *Standards*, such techniques yield one of the five types of validity evidence, evidence about the internal structure of the test. Here, the structure of the data should reflect that of the universe of generalization as unidimensional or as having a certain number of dimensions. In order to conduct analyses of internal structure in support of generalization, the grounds consist of scores that accurately summarize relevant performance, as shown in Figure 5.1. These grounds are the conclusion from the evaluation inference.

Evaluation Inferences for Test Tasks

When an evaluation inference is made, the test scores are trusted as accurately summarizing relevant performance on test tasks. The term *evaluation* is used to encompass the multiple conditions that must hold to warrant such trust, as illustrated in Figure 5.2. The evaluation inference is concerned with the quality of the performance sample at the item or task level whereas a generalization inference comes to a conclusion about the consistency of the total scores. The support for the evaluation inference can be found in many of the good testing practices that underlie operational testing, including the provision of accommodations to ensure fair access to the test for all test takers. Such practices are not necessarily reported in detail to the public. Nevertheless, in the documents for the three tests, sufficient information is provided to reveal how the three types of warrants are addressed.

Warrants for Evaluation Inferences

The first two types of warrants concern the success of the test administration and scoring for obtaining accurate scores. In some tests, as Kane (1992) noted, procedures are specified precisely. "In some attitude and personality inventories and in some tests, the questions and scoring keys are often standardized. The instructions given to examinees and the methods used to generate scores from the raw data are also specified in detail. It is assumed that these standardized procedures are followed exactly" (p. 529). The assumptions underlying these warrants are that the specified procedures are adhered to, but other assumptions are that the procedures

Figure 5.2   Schematic Structure of the Evaluation Inference and Its
Claim and Warrants to Serve as Part of a Validity Argument

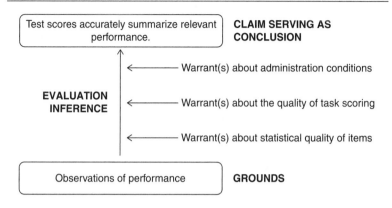

are clearly specified and communicated to test administrators as well as
that the required equipment, software, and troubleshooting procedures are
in place. Moreover, issues of scoring take on an expanded prominence in
the validity argument when automated scoring is used to evaluate test takers' constructed responses (Bennett & Bajar, 1998; Clauser, Kane, &
Swanson, 2002). The second type of warrant can involve additional
assumptions, depending on the nature of the scoring procedures. They state
the appropriateness of the scoring rationale and procedures for scoring the
test tasks. Assumptions include that the scoring rules or rating criteria are
appropriate, that the scoring procedures are applied as specified, and that
item-level scoring is free from bias. A third type of warrant is about the
observed quality of the items based on empirical investigation of characteristics of the test tasks, which refer to both the statistical item characteristics and the qualitative cognitive and performance processes test takers
engage during test taking. The warrants for evaluation inferences are typically attended to by testers as part of initial research and development as
well as ongoing quality assurance processes, as illustrated by the three
example tests.

Assumptions for Evaluation Warrants

Some of the warrants and assumptions underlying an evaluation inference for the MSCEIT are evident in the statements about the acceptability of the item types and their scoring. As part of the test development
and piloting of the MSCEIT, the authors have developed the items to
assess ability rather than affect or judgment (Mayer et al., 2008). Each of
the four aspects of the emotional intelligence construct is assessed using

tasks that are "to-be-solved problems, and test takers' responses can be checked against a criterion of correctness" (p. 507). Scoring for correctness of the responses, in this case, required a warrant stating that a key had been developed from multiple studies investigating expert consensus to specify exact responses (Warrant 2). The assumptions underlying this warrant were that judgments of correct scores given by experts correlated strongly with those of the test takers, the experts participating in the research held sufficient credentials to serve as experts on emotional intelligence, and obtaining consensus on correct responses is recognized as a legitimate method to establish a scoring key in intelligence testing (Mayer et al., 2012).

Educational Testing Service presents information supporting the three types of warrants for the evaluation inference in the public document *Reliability and Comparability of TOEFL iBT^{TM} Scores* (Educational Testing Service, 2011b). Warrant 1 about administration conditions states that test administration is carried out to ensure high levels of

Table 5.4 Summary of Claim, Warrants, and Assumptions for Evaluation Inferences for the MSCEIT

Claim: The MSCEIT scores are an accurate summary of relevant performance on the test tasks.

Warrant About Administration Conditions	*Warrant About the Quality of Task Scoring*
Warrant 1: Task performance requires demonstration of the ability to reason about emotions, which is not susceptible to error introduced by test takers' responses reflecting social desirability.	Warrant 2: Task responses are scored for correctness by using a key developed from multiple studies investigating expert consensus to specify exact responses.
A.1.1 Test items are designed to assess the ability to recognize and use emotions across a range of situations, rather than test takers' perceptions about their probable behavior in situations in which emotional intelligence would be called upon.	A.2.1 Judgments of correct scores given by experts correlated strongly with those of the test takers.
	A.2.2 Experts participating in the research determining response keys held sufficient credentials to serve as experts on emotional intelligence.
	A.2.3 Consensus on correct responses is recognized as a legitimate method to establish a scoring key in intelligence testing.

Table 5.5 Summary of Claim, Warrants, and Assumptions for Evaluation Inferences for the TOEFL iBT

Claim: The TOEFL iBT scores are an accurate summary of relevant performance on the test tasks

Warrant About Administration Conditions	Warrant About the Quality of Task Scoring	Warrant About the Empirical Quality of Task Scores
Warrant 1: Test administration is carried out to ensure high levels of standardization and security as outlined in the *ETS Standards for Quality and Fairness* (Educational Testing Service, 2002).	Warrant 2: The constructed responses on the speaking and writing tasks are rated using procedures to assure agreement between raters.	Warrant 3: Test tasks are selected for inclusion on the test based on their performance in an empirical investigation prior to their use.
A.1.1 A certification process verifies readiness of test centers, their equipment, and internet connections for test administration.	A.2.1 Raters are trained to use well-defined scoring rubrics.	A.3.1 On the listening and reading sections, items are pretested before being selected for a test form and then used as anchors in the equating process.
A.1.2 Test center staff are trained to administer the test according to guidelines (e.g., verifying test taker identity, launching the test, and troubleshooting).	A.2.2 Raters are certified based on their post-training performance.	A.3.2 On the speaking and writing sections, small-scale trials are conducted prior to use.
A.1.3 Test taker preparation is encouraged by providing practice tests and other information to help them become familiar with test-taking conditions.	A.2.3 Raters' expertise is monitored by recalibration prior to each rating session.	A.3.3 On each task of the speaking and writing sections, distributions of average task scores are monitored.
A.1.4. Technology is used to deliver the test securely, mitigate against unauthorized content disclosure, and transmit test results safely.	A.2.4 During rating sessions, raters are supervised and monitored.	
A.1.5. Test takers are given instructions on how they can report suspected cheating during the test session.	A.2.5 Average session ratings from each rater are calculated and compared to all average session ratings.	
	A.2.6. Rater exact and adjacent agreement on task ratings are calculated.	

standardization and security as outlined in the *ETS Standards for Quality and Fairness* (Educational Testing Service, 2002). The assumptions underlying this warrant state the activities in place, including a test center certification process, test center staff training, preparation materials for test takers, technology-assisted security measures, and guidance to test takers for reporting cheating. Warrant 2 states that the constructed responses on the speaking and writing tasks are rated using procedures to assure agreement between raters. The assumptions include the processes for training, certifying, supervising, and monitoring raters and their ratings.

The *Guide* for the Iowa Assessments includes warrants about each of the three types of warrants to authorize the evaluation inference. Warrant 1 stating that tests are administered according to a standardized procedures rests on the assumption that test users adhere to the manual provided by the publisher. Warrant 2 states that correct responses in selected response format are unambiguous and accurately keyed. This warrant is based on the practices undertaken when item data are available from the field testing before they are used in operational testing. By examining the test takers response data, the testers identify any of the alternatives presented in the multiple choice items that were disproportionately mistaken for the correct response as well as double-check the correctness of the keyed responses and their wording. Warrant 3 is that test tasks selected for inclusion on the test based on their content coverage also have desired statistical characteristics. This warrant is based on assumptions about the use of item difficulty, discrimination, and differential item functioning statistics that are calculated from the field testing data.

Threats to Reliability

The many threats to reliability that are apparent from the warrants for evaluation and generalization inferences can form the basis for rebuttals. Table 5.7 provides examples of some of the rebuttals that state potential threats to the quality of the performance sample obtained from test takers on the example tests. One potential threat comes from any deficiencies in procedures for administration or scoring. A second comes from inappropriate or unknown empirical task characteristics, which can refer to both the statistical item characteristics and the cognitive and performance processes test takers use during test taking. A third is the limits of the norming sample

Table 5.6 Summary of Claim, Warrants, and Assumptions for the Evaluation Inference for the Iowa Assessments

Claim: The Iowa Assessments scores are an accurate summary of relevant performance on the test tasks.

Warrant About Administration Conditions	Warrant About the Quality of Task Scoring	Warrant About the Empirical Quality of Task Scores
Warrant 1: Tests are administered according to standardized procedures. A.1.1 A manual containing complete instructions for test administration is supplied to test users. A.1.2 Test users follow the instructions as provided.	Warrant 2: Correct responses in selected response format are unambiguous and accurately keyed. A.2.1 Item-level data from field testing are used to reexamine distractors. A.2.1 Item-level data from field testing are used to help check response keys for accuracy.	Warrant 3: Test tasks selected for inclusion on the test based on their content coverage also have desired statistical characteristics. A.3.1 The test development process includes a field test yielding difficulty and discrimination item statistics, which are taken into account in selecting items for the final test forms. A.3.2 Field test data are used to identify items reflecting systematic differences in performance of subgroups of test takers.

used to gather performance data and make decisions before the test is used operationally. If the norming sample is different from the intended test takers' relevant to the validity argument, decisions about items to include on the final forms of the test are suspect. Accordingly, if the norming sample does not accurately reflect certain of the subpopulations of intended test takers, a general claim for reliability would not be warranted. Investigation of reliability within identified subgroups needs to be carried out to determine any limits to a reliability claim. Fourth, ineffective task specifications negatively affect the production of comparable forms of a test. Any rebuttals placed in a validity argument would invite investigation; concerns expressed as rebuttals are not assumed to be accurate without findings that support their plausibility.

Table 5.7 Examples of Rebuttals That Would Limit the Plausibility of Evaluation Inferences, if Supported

| Example Test | Potential Source of Threat | | | |
	Deficiencies in procedures for administration or scoring	Inappropriate or unknown empirical task characteristics	Limits of the norming sample	Ineffective task specifications
MSCEIT	Test takers get access to test content and correct responses prior to taking the test.	All of the tasks testing recognition of emotions are too easy for intended test takers.	The norming sample of undergraduate students used for reporting reliability limits claims of reliability to this population.	The characteristics of the scenarios are not sufficiently specified for experts to produce parallel tasks.
TOEFL iBT	Ratings conducted in some sessions are not monitored for difficulty levels.	The difficulty of certain writing tasks is inaccurately judged by test developers.	The norming sample overrepresents high-ability students relative to the actual population of test takers.	The degree of technical detail that should appear in reading tasks is not specified sufficiently to select materials of equivalent reading difficulty.
Iowa Assessments	In some testing sites, insufficient time is given to students needing this accommodation.	At the low levels, too many of the mathematics items are too difficult.	The norming sample includes students experienced in taking the Iowa Assessments, whereas the testing population includes a wider variety of test takers.	Specifications for creating computer-delivered versions of mathematics tasks do not result in equivalent tasks to the paper-based tasks.

Conclusion

In writing about the MSCEIT, Mayer et al. (2003) summed up the relationship among evaluation, generalization, and explanation inferences: "One must know how to score a tests' items before one can settle such issues as the test's reliability and factor structure" (p. 98). Similarly, the *Research and Development Guide* for the Iowa Assessments, introduces Part 7 on Item and Test Analysis with the point that obtaining a high reliability of scores requires pretesting items to determine the difficulty and discrimination of the items in order to choose the ones that will best contribute to reliability. Argument-based validity takes these sentiments into account through the hierarchical positioning of the evaluation, generalization, and explanation inferences. At the bottom of the hierarchy are the warrants of the evaluation inference with the assumptions about test administration, scoring, and observed properties of items. Their assumptions must be met to draw any conclusions about the quality of the data that are used in subsequent analyses to provide evidence for reliability. In turn, assumptions underlying warrants about generalization must be met to draw a positive conclusion about the consistency reflected in the scores. Reliable scores serve as the grounds for making an inference about the test construct because a construct is a meaningful interpretation of performance consistency. Prior to these three inferences, test users infer that the test content has been properly defined and developed. The warrants and assumptions that underlie the inference about the quality of test development is the topic of the next chapter.

Chapter 6

CONTENT DOMAIN-RELATED INFERENCE: DOMAIN DEFINITION

This chapter explains how the test development process can be included in a validity argument. Valid score interpretations and uses rest on the quality of the test content, the material that testers include on the test, the task types and their configuration, as well as the test length and administration procedures. Any validity argument is built—at least implicitly—on the grounds of test development rationales and processes. Argument-based validity provides the tools for explicitly expressing the inferences that score users make about test development whenever they interpret and use test scores. Test development is itself an extensive topic, which the *Standards* presents in a chapter separate from the one on validity, but the chapter on validity also includes analysis of test content as one of the five sources of validity evidence. Building on the uncontroversial position taken in the *Standards* that test content is important for validity, this chapter examines the warrants about test content that serve as support for a domain definition inference in a validity argument. The three example tests are used to demonstrate how a variety of content development issues support the domain definition inference.

Test Development in Validity Arguments

Historically, test content, and therefore the process of its creation, has been a fundamental validity concern resulting in testers coining the expression *content validity* to denote the need "to guard against strictly numerical evaluations of tests and other measures that overlooked serious threats to the validity of inferences derived from their scores" (Sireci, 1998a, p. 83). Content validity as a separate type of validity, however, is problematic. Messick (1989) dispensed with the expression *content validity* in his unitary definition of validity because he saw test content as central to construct validity, which for him was the cornerstone for validity. He explained the danger in conceptualizing evaluation of content validity as a separate or even an alternative to what some testers saw as other types (criterion-related and construct validity). In short, Messick saw test content as too important to be relegated a status outside the main concerns of validation.

Similarly, before Messick, test content had always played an important role in validation. For Cureton (1951), test content was part of the relevance of a test, which was one of his two aspects of validity. Cronbach (1971) saw test content as part of the operational definition of the construct and as essential for descriptive interpretations of test scores. Like Cronbach, Kane (2002) has referred to the quality of test content for making descriptive interpretations of test scores. For example, what he calls "semantic inferences" are supported by statements that refer to (1) the fidelity of the test specifications to the standards that are used to characterize the target domain and (2) the representativeness of the test content to the target domain. Overall, however, Kane's presentations of argument-based validity focus on the inferences required to build an interpretation from an observation on a test task to the uses and consequences of the test scores. Kane's example validity arguments make an implicit inference about the quality of the test development processes guiding the design and creation of the assessment tasks that are appropriate for eliciting test takers' performance. For many testers, however, this process of defining the domain to be tested is the basis of all other inferences, and therefore should be stated explicitly to serve as the foundation for the validity argument. It is therefore worthwhile to examine the meaning of the domain definition inference and the types of warrants and assumptions that can be used for its support.

The Domain Definition Inference

A domain definition inference is made in a validity argument when a claim is stated about the quality of the test development process for obtaining observations of performance that are appropriate for the intended interpretations and uses of the test. To develop the types of warrants and assumptions that support a domain definition inference, Kane's presentation of validity argument is augmented by the extensive study of content validity by Sireci (1998a, 1998b) and aspects of the evidence-centered design (ECD) framework for test development created by Mislevy, Steinberg, and Almond (2003). ECD makes explicit the processes and products of test design that can be used in support of the domain definition inferences in a validity argument, as illustrated by Chapelle et al. (2018). ECD capitalizes on the fact that "test developers always have crafted tasks from implicit theories of context, drawing on their understandings of the targeted domains, test takers, and intended uses" of tests (Mislevy, 2018, p. 81). Both of these sources rely extensively on the concepts of the test domain (also referred to as the "assessment domain") and the target domain to conceptualize issues of content in test development.

Even though the term *domain* has long been used in the discussion of test development, it requires a bit more clarity before it can usefully serve in argument-based validity.

What Is a Domain?

The term *domain*, like the word *construct* in educational and psychological assessment, is used in many and various ways. A domain is an area of knowledge, content, theory, practice, or interest that is demarcated because of its social significance or utility. For example, mathematics is one domain within the school curriculum, which is used for talking about learning outcomes or students' achievement. Mathematics would be widely recognized as an established educationally important domain, but the abstract concept of a domain such as mathematics is not static. It can evolve, and it can be defined in different ways by developers of curricula, teaching materials, and tests across levels and contexts. Domains are spaces that are not naturally occurring but that are formed by volition, sometimes by an author within a text to explain theoretical concepts or make clear to a community the intended boundaries of an area to guide practical work. Validation research uses both the abstract concept of a domain as an area of recognized importance (e.g., mathematics) and the more technical meaning of an area demarcated for clarity within a community (e.g., the mathematics curriculum in a particular school district).

Two senses of domain needed for expressing warrants and assumptions in a validity argument are the test domain and the target domain, which are represented schematically in Figure 6.1 as they relate to the test construct. Figure 6.1. is a simplified and adapted rendering of Messick's (1989) schematic diagram of a "constructive-realist view" (p. 30) of constituents required to conceptualize validation. On the left side, the test domain, represented as the rectangle, appears as the domain in which test performance is elicited. Test performance refers to the observed performance, or responses to test tasks, on an occasion of testing. The particular tasks on a test are created and selected on the basis of test specifications, which define the test domain. The Iowa Assessments *Guide* even uses the term *domain specifications* for test specifications. The test domain is not a single form of a test itself; rather, it is a description of all of the types of tasks that could appear on the test and the rules for organizing them. In argument-based validity, the test domain is also referred to as the "universe of generalization," as introduced in Chapter 5.

On the right side of Figure 6.1, the target domain is portrayed as the domain in which performance in nontesting contexts takes place. The target domain was introduced in Chapter 4, in the claim that the TOEFL iBT

Figure 6.1   Relationships Among Domains as Conceptualized During
Test Development

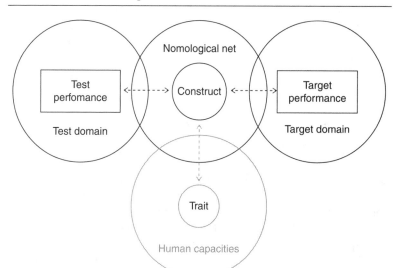

scores are relevant to English-language performance in an academic context. Performance in a target (nontest) domain is always the interest of testers, and the observed test performance is only a sample of such performances. The dotted double arrow between the target performance and the construct denotes that the construct is responsible for the target performance, which is, accordingly, interpreted as a manifestation of the construct. This dotted double arrow on the left (between construct and test performance) marks the conceptual positioning of the explanation inference. The dotted double arrow between the construct and the target performance marks the conceptual positioning of the extrapolation inference in a validity argument with both inferences.

A third use of the term *domain* appears in discussion of test development, particularly for tests with a trait-type construct such as emotional intelligence. Such tests rely on the theoretical construct definition, which is expected to be relevant across a wide range of target domains, to create test specifications. In such cases, domain refers to the construct itself. A trait-type construct is theorized to be applicable across a wide range of contexts; therefore, a target context cannot be defined for the purposes of test development. Instead, the details provided in the construct representation (i.e., the internal components of the trait) serve in test development. A good rule of thumb as a consumer of test development documents is to avoid attributing any technical meaning to the term *domain* unless it appears with a modifier such as "test" or "assessment," "target," or "construct." When the term is used unmodified, the author may mean any one of these technical entities in testing or something altogether different, such as "subject area." As developers of validity arguments, testers are advised to make the meaning of domain clear by using these modifiers in expressing claims, warrants, rebuttals, and assumptions.

Warrants and Assumptions for Domain Definition

The aspects of test development that should be taken into account in a validity argument are largely what the *Standards* refers to as "evidence based on the content of the test." Sireci's thorough historical and methodological study of content validity adds important background to the statement in the *Standards*, and Sireci and Faulkner-Bond (2014) have provided detail that is useful for conceptualizing how content evidence for validity can help to formulate relevant warrants and assumptions for a domain definition inference. As shown in Figure 6.2, three of the four warrants for domain definition make direct reference to the test domain, the target domain, or both.

The first type of warrant is a statement about the quality of the descriptions of the target domain and the test domain. Target domains are complex, multi-faceted, and unique to particular test development contexts. The complexity of target domains and the need for defensible analysis methods prompted the development of ECD to aid in test development. The systematic process undertaken in test development serves as support for the assumptions underlying domain definition. Sireci and Faulkner-Bond (2014) summarized the assumptions as follows: (1) Experts agree that the target domain has been described in a manner that is consistent with current perspectives in the field and relevant to the test purpose, (2) experts agree that the test domain accurately reflects the target domain in a manner that allows for creation of test tasks, and (3) the description of the test domain explicitly acknowledges the aspects of the target domain not covered in the test domain.

The second type of warrant states that the test adequately represents the target and test domains. One assumption is that the items selected for each form of a test adequately sample from the test domain. To investigate this assumption, experts can be given a rubric for analysis of test items and asked to evaluate each item relative to the test specifications. Another assumption is that the tasks specified in the test domain and appearing on any form of the test align with the target domain description. Backing for

Figure 6.2 Warrants Supporting a Domain Definition Inference in a
Validity Argument

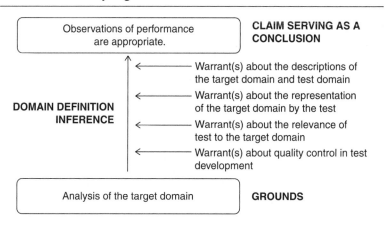

this assumption is sought in alignment studies, which elicit expert judgment about the quality of each item for assessing its intended aspect of the target domain (Sireci & Faulkner-Bond, 2014). The aspect of the target domain could be stated as standards, course objectives, task characteristics, or other features depending on the outcomes of the domain analysis process.

The third type of warrant is a statement about the relevance of each item on a test to the test and target domains. Whereas representation refers to the adequacy of the tasks for covering the breadth of the test and target domain, relevance concerns how appropriate the tasks are in requiring performance that is relevant to the target domain. Therefore, one assumption is that the test tasks are relevant to the target domain. Another assumption is that the content and cognitive demands of the test tasks are relevant to those defined in the test specifications, which reflect the test domain. Expert opinion about the representativeness and relevance of the test tasks to the test and target domains take account of the issues connected to content evidence for validity. Accordingly, methodologies for systematically obtaining expert judgments about these assumptions have a long history in testing (Sireci & Faulkner-Bond, 2014).

The fourth type of warrant is a statement about the processes for quality control in test development. Sireci and Faulkner-Bond (2014) identified assumptions about quality control processes as the following: (1) There is a procedure in place to review, modify, and/or discard test tasks for matters of content and technical quality; (2) the review procedure ensures that the test does not contain material that may be considered offensive, advantageous, or disadvantageous to certain test takers while being nonessential for representing the target domain; (3) a process is in place during test development for piloting, statistically analyzing the results, and acting on the results to modify and/or discard test tasks; and (4) a process is in place during test development and operational testing for continued statistical analysis, including differential item functioning (DIF) analysis for identifying test tasks that disadvantage particular subgroups of test takers. Responsible test publishers maintain elaborate processes for quality control of items, as described in the *ETS Guidelines for Fair Tests and Communications*. Such processes are important for eliminating test content that unfairly disadvantages individual or groups of test takers.

These general warrants and assumptions about the quality of test development offer guidelines for recognizing the importance of test development processes as the foundation for a validity argument. Such practices typically occur behind the scenes for professional testing programs, and their detail is therefore not always discernible in the publicly available information. Nevertheless, sufficient discussion of test development is provided for each of the three example tests to provide examples of how the warrants and assumptions for the domain definition inference in their respective validity arguments could be expressed.

Domain Definition for the Example Tests

The three example tests encompass a range of test purposes and contexts for test development. They therefore illustrate different approaches to their respective target domains. The target domain for the Iowa Assessments consisted of what is taught to students in public schools in the United States. The academic content as analyzed and planned for each grade level was important for development of the achievement tests. The target domain for the TOEFL iBT was also the academic context. As an admissions test for English-medium universities, the domain consists of academic tasks requiring students to use English for learning. This domain had not been analyzed and presented as curriculum documents that could serve in the domain analysis, so the test developers undertook a domain analysis process that worked with the raw materials of academic tasks. The target domain of the MSCEIT was the theoretical construct of emotional intelligence as it had been defined by the researchers in their previous work. Despite the different approaches to target domains required across the three test development contexts, some common warrants and assumptions about the quality of the test development process are evident.

Iowa Assessments

The *Research and Development Guide* for the Iowa Assessments emphasizes the importance of the test development process by naming content evidence as one of five sources of validity evidence and by explaining the test development processes. All four types of warrants for a domain definition inference are stated and support for their corresponding assumptions is provided, as summarized in Table 6.1. Warrant 1, that the target domain is described appropriately for the test purpose, is supported with a description of the domain analysis. This domain analysis included investigation of national and state standards, curricula and materials, and teachers' views about the importance of content in their teaching. Other support would come from a demonstration of the utility of the analysis for creating the test specifications.

Warrant 2 is that the test tasks adequately represent the target domain, as defined in the test specifications. One assumption is that the test specifications state the appropriate proportions of content, skills to be tested, and levels of cognitive engagement required to reflect the target domain. The second assumption is that the test specifications provide sufficient detail to serve as a blueprint for creating test forms that accurately represent the target domain. The third assumption is that the test specifications require development of more items than required for creating tests, to allow for an item review process that eliminates inadequate items. Warrant 3 is that the test is free of irrelevant content, sources of difficulty, and cognitive demands. The two assumptions state the review processes consisting of both expert content reviews and item analysis from pretest results. Warrant 4 is that the development process includes a high degree of quality control. Assumptions provide detail about the practices assumed to uphold quality standards including creating more items than needed, multiple reviews targeting potential known problems, field testing, and statistical item analysis including DIF analysis.

TOEFL iBT

TOEFL iBT Test Framework and Test Development introduces the target domain by stating that the TOEFL is intended to test the "ability of international students to use English in an academic environment" (Educational Testing Service, 2010). Despite steering clear of the term *domain,* the

Table 6.1 Summary of Claim, Four Warrants, and Assumptions for the Domain Definition Inference for the Iowa Assessments.

Claim: The observations of performance on the test tasks are appropriate for the educational purposes of the Iowa Assessments.

Warrant About Descriptions of Target and Test Domains	Warrant About Representation of Target and Test Domains	Warrant About Relevance to Target and Test Domains	Warrant About Quality Control Processes
Warrant 1: The domain that the test is intended to assess is described appropriately for the test purpose.	Warrant 2: The test tasks adequately represent the domain, as defined in the test specifications.	Warrant 3: The test is free of irrelevant content, sources of difficulty, and cognitive demands.	Warrant 4: The development process includes a high degree of quality control.
A.1.1 The target domain of subject area curricula was described appropriately by examining the Common Core State Standards, individual state standards, curriculum guidelines, and classroom materials, as well as by conducting teacher surveys.	A.2.1 Test forms adhere to the test specifications that state the appropriate proportions of content, skills to be tested, and levels of cognitive engagement required.	A.3.1 Draft items are reviewed internally and externally to flag items containing irrelevant content, potential bias, and level inappropriate demands.	A.4.1 Standard practice requires writing more items that required for test creation, as well as reviewing, modifying, and discarding items based on content and/or statistical review.
A.1.2 Test specifications were created based on the analysis of these multiple sources to convey the content of the test and its organization.	A.2.2 Test specifications provide sufficient detail to serve as a blueprint for creating test forms that accurately represent the target domain.	A.3.2 Items are field tested to obtain item statistics that are reviewed to identify items with potentially irrelevant content.	A.4.2 The process for item development includes multiple reviews by different trained item reviewers charged with identifying nonessential content that may disadvantage a certain subgroup of test takers.
A.1.3 Ongoing review of the target domain and revision of test specifications keep their description up to date.	A.2.3 Test specifications require development of more items than required for creating tests, to allow for an item review process that eliminates inadequate items while maintaining the test specifications.		A.4.3 Items are field tested and results of the item statistics are used to eliminate items and create test forms adhering to content and statistical specifications.
			A.4.4 Item analysis, including DIF analysis, is conducted on operational forms to monitor item quality.

Note: DIF = differential item functioning

document refers to the academic environment, which is the target domain for purposes of test development. Test development was guided by an ECD process (Mislevy et al., 2003), which served as support for the domain definition inference as described by Chapelle et al. (2008). The first steps in the ECD process were to conduct an analysis of the target domain relevant for test score interpretation and to define the key characteristics of that domain, which would serve in defining the test domain. The warrants and assumptions for the domain definition inference in the TOEFL iBT validity argument are summarized in Table 6.2.

The first steps of the ECD process and their results serve as backing for Warrant 1, which states that the domain that the test is intended to assess is described appropriately for the test purpose. The assumptions are that the domain analysis identified important language tasks required in English-medium universities (Rosenfeld, Leung, & Oltman, 2001), that it described the linguistic characteristics of academic language tasks (Biber et al., 2004), and that it provided sufficient descriptive information to create useful test specifications. Warrant 2 is that the test tasks adequately represent the domain as defined in the test specifications and the target domain. The assumptions are that the test tasks adhere to the test framework, creating tests with four sections; each of the four sections is created according to the test assembly specifications; and items adhere to standards for reflecting academic English as defined in the target domain.

Warrant 3 states that the test is free of irrelevant content. Assumptions are that item writers adhere to item writing guidelines to create materials at the appropriate level of difficulty, free from the need for specific academic background knowledge and avoiding culturally inaccessible topics. Warrant 4 states that the development process includes practices to maintain a high degree of quality control. Assumptions cover a range of quality control practices, such as qualifications and training of item writers; multistage content review of test content, including consideration of content effects on test takers from different cultural backgrounds; pretesting or piloting items with selected or constructed responses; and monitoring performance of items on operational test forms. The support for the assumptions, therefore, is found in the specifications of quality control processes as well as investigations, or audits, of how they are carried out and of their success.

MSCEIT

The developers of the MSCEIT refer to the test as assessing "the domain of EI" (e.g., Mayer et al., 2003, p. 98). This use of the term *domain* appears in Mayer et al.'s (2016) paper about the MSCEIT as they state the importance of the test content: "If the test content is poorly specified, the items

Table 6.2 Summary of Claim, Warrants, and Assumptions for the Domain Definition Inference for the TOEFL iBT

Claim: The observations of performance on the test tasks reveal relevant knowledge, skills, and abilities in situations representative of those in the target domain of language use in English-medium institutions of higher education.

Warrant About Descriptions of Target and Test Domains	Warrant About Representation of Target and Test Domains	Warrant About Relevance to Target and Test Domains	Warrant About Quality Control Processes
Warrant 1: The domain that the test is intended to assess is described appropriately for the test purpose.	Warrant 2: The test tasks adequately represent the domain, as defined in the test specifications.	Warrant 3: The test is free of irrelevant content.	Warrant 4: The development process includes practices to maintain a high degree of quality control.
A.1.1 The domain analysis identified important language tasks required in English medium universities.	A.2.1 The test tasks adhere to the test framework, creating tests with four sections.	A.3.1 Item writers adhere to guidelines specifying that items are constructed using materials at the appropriate level of difficulty without content that is cognitively or culturally inaccessible.	A.4.1 Item writers are well qualified and trained on the targeted characteristics of the desired test items.
A.1.2 The domain analysis described the linguistic characteristics of academic language tasks.	A.2.2 Within each of the four test sections, test forms are created according to the test assembly specifications.	A.3.2 Item writers adhere to guidelines specifying that items use materials that do not require specific academic background knowledge to be comprehensible.	A.4.2 Items undergo a multistage content review resulting in modification or elimination of inadequate materials.
A.1.3 The domain analysis yielded sufficient descriptive information to create useful test specifications.	A.2.3 All test items adhere to standards for reflecting academic English as defined in the target domain.		A.4.3 Items deemed to offend or unfairly advantage or disadvantage any subpopulation of test takers are flagged in review and eliminated from the test.
			A.4.4 Items on the reading and listening sections are pretested, and the statistical results are taken into account for their possible inclusion on operational tests.
			A.4.5 Speaking and writing tasks undergo small-scale piloting to gather evidence about their viability for producing scorable performance.
			A.4.5 Items on operational tests are monitored statistically and questionable findings are acted upon.

will misrepresent the domain" (p. 292). The trait-type construct of emotional intelligence that underlies the intended score meaning for the MSCEIT does not suggest a target domain like that of the Iowa Assessments or the TOEFL iBT. A trait-type construct is assumed to be relevant to performance in a wide range of target domains; therefore, the MSCEIT development process could not begin with the same type of analysis of a target domain as the other tests did. Instead, when a test is developed to assess a trait-type construct such as the MSCEIT, the term *domain* is used to refer to the construct itself—in this case, emotional intelligence. In other words, for the researchers the target domain is the construct. The research

Table 6.3 Summary of Claim, Warrants, and Assumptions for the Domain Definition Inference for the MSCEIT

Claim: The observations of performance on the MSCEIT tasks are appropriate to the test purpose.

Warrant About Descriptions of Target and Test Domains[1]	*Warrant About Representation of Target and Test Domains*	*Warrant About Test Relevance to Target and Test Domains*
Warrant 1: The construct domain that the test is intended to assess is described appropriately for the test purpose.	Warrant 2: The test tasks adequately represent the domain as defined in the test specifications.	Warrant 3: The test is free of irrelevant content.
A.1.1 The domain of emotional intelligence has been theorized incrementally through empirical testing.	A.2.1 The test tasks are designed to test problem-solving ability in four areas defined in test specifications.	A.3.1 The test tasks are designed to test problem-solving ability as specified in the domain theory of emotional intelligence.
A.1.2 Theory and research have identified four components of ability that define the construct of emotional intelligence	A.2.2 Within each of the four areas, two different response formats are used to represent the domain, to minimize systematic error from method effects.	A.3.2 Test tasks are free from items assessing attitudes, emotions, or judgments.
A.1.3 Test specifications are designed to sample problem-solving ability in each of the four domains of emotional intelligence.		

[1]The construct domain of emotional intelligence is treated as the target domain for the MSCEIT because emotional intelligence is a trait-type construct.

papers do not specify the precise basis for the test specifications, but some of the warrants for a domain definition inference are evident in their discussion of the test, as shown in Table 6.3.

Warrant 1 states that the construct domain that the test is intended to assess is described appropriately for the test purpose. One assumption states that the theoretical definition of emotional intelligence has been developed through a synergistic program of theory, test development, and empirical testing. A second assumption states that theory and research have identified four components of ability that make up emotional intelligence, as defined in Chapter 4. A third assumption states that the construct theory was used to develop test specifications, which indicate how to create tasks that sample problem-solving ability in each of the four domains of emotional intelligence. Warrant 2 is that the test tasks adequately represent the domain as defined in the test specifications. The assumptions are that the test tasks are designed to test problem-solving ability in four areas specified in test specifications and that two different response formats are used to represent the domain, to minimize systematic error from method effects. Warrant 3 asserts that the test is free of irrelevant content. The assumptions underlying this warrant are that the test tasks are designed to test problem-solving ability as specified in the domain theory of emotional intelligence and that test tasks are free from items assessing attitudes, emotions, or judgments. The distinction the researchers make between emotional intelligence as reasoning about emotions as opposed to affective responses to emotion is important for creating tasks that assess the construct as they have defined it for the MSCEIT. The rigor that may characterize the test development process is not specified in the research papers, but presumably the researchers could specify a fourth warrant with assumptions about the technical quality of the test development process and its monitoring.

The use of the term *domain* to refer to theoretically important but different concepts across test development contexts is perhaps a good example of Norris's (1983, p. 69) critique of educational and psychological testing. However, given the range of participants in the field and their varied theories and purposes, it may be more fruitful to find common ground than it would be to seek common language in this case. The common ground is the unequivocal acceptance of the position that valid score interpretations and uses of test scores rest on the quality of the actual test items or tasks that test takers are asked to perform. The domain that serves as grounds for the domain definition inference is therefore the foundation upon which the validity argument is built. The domain does not have to mean the same thing across different test contexts, but it needs to mean something specific in each test context.

Conclusion

The relevance of test content in a validity argument can be seen across multiple different inferences. Test specifications and scoring appear in the assumptions underlying evaluation and generalization whose warrants and assumptions refer to equivalence across tasks and forms, clarity of scoring rubrics, and quality of items. Content can also come into play in assumptions underlying explanation and extrapolation in assumptions about the construct and target domains. However, these appearances of content issues are fragmented and considered from the perspective of content already developed. The domain definition inference provides a place in the validity argument to identify the many carefully reasoned rationales, labored development work, quality control measures, and ongoing content analysis that underlies valid interpretations and uses of tests. It also creates a space for identifying rebuttals based on concerns about inadequate test development processes resulting in inappropriate content for all or a subgroup of test takers. The final chapter places the domain definition inference in its cornerstone position in the validity argument, with all of the inferences in their respective positions scaffolding upward to a conclusion about consequences.

Chapter 7

BUILDING A VALIDITY ARGUMENT

This chapter presents guidance for readers who want to develop a validity argument. It begins by summarizing how the claims introduced in the previous chapters are connected logically, each by serving as a conclusion for one inference and as grounds for the next inference. The rest of the chapter outlines how testers can create their own validity arguments. It first conceptualizes the sociocultural milieu of validation in which testers play various roles in developing and evaluating validity arguments, which serve as instruments for planning and communication. These roles for validity arguments provide the background for understanding the contingent nature of validity arguments. The development process is outlined for two contingencies, one an existing test and the other a new test. Three stages of validity argument development are outlined: formulating the interpretation use argument, conducting the validation research, and integrating results into a validity argument.

The Logic of Validity Arguments

Each of the past four chapters introduced one or two types of claims that serve as conclusions for particular inferences in a validity argument. In some cases, readers could undoubtedly see direct parallels between the inferences and familiar concepts in measurement. For example, the inferences of evaluation and generalization each encompass certain aspects of reliability. Inferences of explanation and extrapolation cover issues similar to those addressed in research on construct validity. The domain definition inference requires support from practices carried out as part of test development. Each chapter has shown how stating certain warrants and assumptions helps to explicate each inference by identifying the types of evidence, or backing, required for supporting their conclusions. The practice of providing detailed warrants and assumptions within a validity argument precludes the puzzling interpretations that sometimes appear in validation research. In argument-based validity, research must be interpreted in view of the role it plays in supporting or failing to support assumptions for warrants or rebuttals in the validity argument. Providing language for specifying inferences, warrants, rebuttals, and assumptions that make up the content of the previous chapters, then, is one important contribution of argument-based validity.

The other major contribution is the explicit logic that links these statements in a validity argument. Using the seven inferences introduced in previous chapters, Figure 7.1 illustrates how each one serves in a validity argument to connect claims to the next to express the logical progression of the validity argument. The argument is intended to make explicit the inferences that score users make when they use test scores. Each inference leads to a specific claim about the test scores. Reading the validity argument diagram therefore might best begin with the claim about the test scores, that is, that the test yields scores that accurately summarize test performance. The diagram shows that accurate test scores are indeed the beginning point, or grounds, for five inferences, but they also are the result, or conclusion, of the evaluation inference. The evaluation inference can be made if there is sufficient support, or backing, for assumptions underlying warrants about administration conditions, the quality of task scoring, and the statistical quality of the items (see Chapter 5). The grounds for the evaluation inference are the appropriate observations of test performance, which serve as the conclusion from the domain definition inference. The domain definition inference requires support from test development processes that can be stated as warrants about the description of the target and test domains, the representation of the target domain by the test, the relevance of the test to the target domain, and quality control in test development (see Chapter 6). The grounds for the domain definition inference consist of the analysis of the target domain that is relevant to score use.

The accurate test scores are the grounds for the generalization inference, which requires support for assumptions underlying warrants about consistency across test forms, consistency across test tasks and their configuration, consistency of ratings, and consistency across testing occasions. If generalization is warranted, the conclusion is that the scores capture performance consistency, making the explanation of test scores or their extrapolation to the target domain worthy of investigation. As explained in Chapter 4, reliable test scores can be interpreted as traits, by stating an explanation inference about a construct; as samples of performance, by stating an extrapolation inference about performance in the target domain; or as both, by including both inferences in the validity argument. The order of the explanation inference prior to the extrapolation inference in Figure 7.1 denotes that in this argument, the conclusion about the test assessing the intended construct is intended to serve as grounds for the inference about target performance.

The conclusion about the scores reflecting performance in the target domain, or target performance, serves as grounds for the utilization inference, which requires support for assumptions underlying warrants about the utility of test scores and the decision rules for using the scores. If the utilization inference is warranted, the conclusion that the test scores are useful

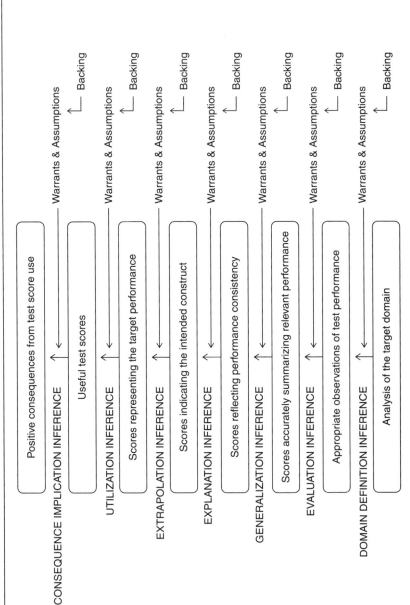

104

Figure 7.1 Schematic Diagram of the Overall Structure of a Validity Argument Containing Seven Claims and Inferences

serves as the grounds for the consequence implication, which is warranted by support for assumptions underlying warrants about benefits to users and benefits to society. Any of these inferences can be limited in scope or shown to be unwarranted by a credible rebuttal (not pictured in Figure 7.1). Rebuttals introduce complications for making one or more claims for all test takers, individual test takers under certain circumstances, or particular subgroups of test takers. When a rebuttal is supported by evidence, the validity argument cannot be made, or must be specified as pertaining only to groups not included in the rebuttal. In this way, validity arguments are intended to be refined based on data that takes into account for whom and under what circumstances test interpretations and uses are valid. As Lenz and Wester (2017) put it, judgments about validity "should be made in consideration of the totality of relevant evidence in juxtaposition to characteristics representing the intersection of setting and population" (p. 203).

The technical concepts expressed by claims, inferences, warrants, rebuttals, and assumptions have their roots in the academic community of educational and psychological testing, but they need to serve in the wider context where tests are developed and used. An understanding of argument-based validity then requires moving from the pages where validity arguments have been sketched by others into the contexts where validity arguments are drafted, disputed, and reformulated for different audiences. Cronbach's (1988) recognition of the importance of the sociocultural milieu for validation motivated his invitation for testers to think of validity argument: Validation research is associated with science and laboratories whereas arguments suggest audiences.

The Sociocultural Milieu of Validation

Kane's (2006) chapter in *Educational Measurement* placed validation in its social context, where claims are made about test scores and their prospective uses, and where such claims are expected to be supported by plausible arguments. He wrote, "Ultimately, the need for validation derives from the scientific and social requirement that public claims and decisions be justified" (p. 17). In this social arena, where the actors as well as their motives, knowledge and biases come into play, the result in many countries has been public debate about testing. In the United States, "legal and methodological debates centered on questions of validity" (Kane, 2016, p. 204). Kane's depiction of the courts as the locus for presentation of validity arguments is useful because it portrays testers as actors who communicate with not only a friendly and knowledgeable audience but also with other actors who may hold different points of view. The courtroom scenario was also evoked by Shepard (2016) in her defense of the consensus view of validity "to communicate with other professionals, courts and judges, parents and other test users" (p. 271). Educational and psychological testing in the courts is a large and complex topic, but Kane's and Shepard's perspectives underscore the various audiences for validity arguments, and the use of validity arguments as a tool for communication within certain communities.

Discourse Communities

A tester is unlikely to enact the role of a lawyer or expert witness all the time, if at all. Instead, testers play multiple roles as they communicate within and across particular discourse communities, which are "sociorhetorical communities that form in order to work towards sets of common goals" (Swales, 1990, p. 9). The word *discourse,* used to modify *community,* refers to oral or written language used in accomplishing objectives. Discourse community denotes the role of communication (rather than, e.g., geography, religion, or demographics) in defining and maintaining coherence within a community that shares interests and purpose through the use of language. Figure 7.2 shows three discourse communities in which validity arguments may serve as the genre for communication about the quality and appropriateness of a test. Genres are "classes of communicative events," (Swales, 1990, p. 9) or ways of selecting and structuring language to accomplish certain goals. For example, in the genre of a service encounter in a drug store in Ontario, certain linguistic moves are undertaken to accomplish a purchase. Other genres include novels, sermons, doctor visits, and editorial blogs.

The smallest circle in Figure 7.2 depicts a discourse community consisting of a team of one or more testers working on developing, maintaining, administering, and marketing one or more tests. Discourse communities share a common language and understanding of what they are doing in part because of the historical and cultural context or tradition that has enacted similar functions in the past. In educational and psychological assessment, this history, sketched in the first chapter, provides critical background knowledge for all testers because it is the basis for their communication among one another.

The three discourse communities in Figure 7.2 overlap with one another, each with porous boundaries symbolized by dotted lines, and within the larger public. The public refers to people without necessarily any interest or knowledge in testing who may at any time be affected by testing and may or may not develop an interest. Shepard's (2016) "courts and judges,

Figure 7.2   Schematic Diagram of Communication Within a Team of
Testers and Across Discourse Communities and the Public

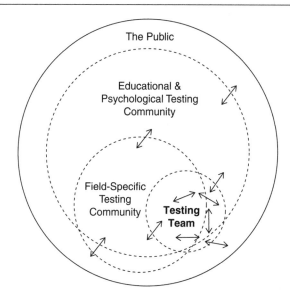

parents and other test users" all make up the public. The largest professional discourse community pictured in Figure 7.2 is made up of the academic and professional community of educational and psychological
testing, represented most clearly by the National Council on Measurement
in Education but consisting of other testing professionals as well. Smaller
communities also exist at the intersection of testing and a particular academic area; they are represented by journals such as *Language Testing,
Measurement and Evaluation in Counseling and Development,* and *Measurement in Physical Education and Exercise Science.* The smallest discourse community shown in Figure 7.2 is a team of testers who develops
the validity arguments for their tests. Each member of such a team brings a
variety of expertise that needs to be communicated with other team members as well as with members of the larger discourse communities where
some of them may have been educated and socialized. Testers also need to
be able to communicate with the public. Resituating validation from the
scientific laboratory to professional discourse communities and public discourse as Cronbach (1988) did highlights the need for communicating an
understanding of what validation is and how it is accomplished.

The Roles of Testers

Many testers may find it difficult to see themselves preparing for their day in court. Cronbach (1988) offered what may seem a more fitting metaphor: "Ideally, validators will prepare as debaters do. Studying a topic from all angles, a debater grasps the arguments pro and con so well that he or she could speak to either side" (p. 3). The debater analogy is useful, but to be more precise about the testers' roles, specifics of the testing contexts also need to be taken into account. In particular, is a tester serving as an internal team member or as an external evaluator? Is the test being created as a new test development project, or does it already exist? Taking into account these two dimensions, Table 7.1 shows on the horizontal axis two distinct positions a tester can occupy with respect to the testing team. On the vertical axis are the two stages of test construction for which a validity argument would be created. The cells contain the names of positions a tester might take in each of the four contexts.

The internal versus external positioning of testers in the two columns of Table 7.1 corresponds with the two uses of the term *validation* that are widely acknowledged in the academic literature (e.g., Kane, 2006, p. 17). Testers internal to a testing program tend to be concerned with developing validity arguments to support interpretations and uses of their tests. Their validity arguments can be seen as confirmationist because they present support for the validity of particular interpretations and uses, although rebuttals can play a role in developing a confirmationist validity argument, particularly to improve test items and identifying limits for

Table 7.1 Example Roles of Testers Serving as Internal Team Members and External Evaluators

	Example Roles of Testers	
Stage of Test	*Internal Team Members*	*External Evaluators*
Existing	• Director of testing program • Marketing and communications • Validation officer • Content developer • Statistical analyst • Technology expert	• External consultant • Academic analyst • Expert witness
New	• Director of R&D • Researchers • Prototype developers	• External consultant

Note: R&D = research and development.

claims. The goal for members of a testing team is to attempt to assemble a credible, evidence-based argument for the intended interpretations and uses of the test. Team members may develop and present an argument for an existing test to improve communication within and beyond the team and to strengthen the basis for the research program. They may also be responsible for creating a new or revised test through a systematic research program that will serve in communication about the intended test use.

Testers external to a testing program may evaluate proposed interpretations and uses by taking up arguments on both or either of the sides of the debate. For example, an external consultant might be contracted to investigate whether or not support exists for rebuttals that have appeared in statements made by members of the public about the inadequacy of the test. An external consultant might also be tasked with conducting research that is expected to result in positive evidence in support of assumptions. In a test development project, an external consultant may even be contracted to help shape the initial interpretation/use argument to guide the research efforts. Academic analysts may take any stance that is interesting and relevant to their research and may therefore hypothesize warrants and assumptions and/or rebuttals as a way of framing their research. An expert witness may be asked to give an opinion on any one or some combination of warrants or rebuttals depending on the nature of the controversy that brings the validity of the test use to court.

Of course, Table 7.1 oversimplifies stages of tests and the positioning of testers, both of which are more fluid than the dichotomies suggest. Nevertheless, this simplified view is useful for looking at the different types of heuristics that serve testers when they develop validity arguments in a variety of situations.

Developing a Validity Argument

Chapter 1 introduced argument-based validation as consisting of three stages. In the first stage, the tester identifies the claims required to make the intended interpretations and uses of the test scores, the inferences that lead to the claims, the warrants that license the inferences, and the assumptions underlying the warrants. This detailed statement of interconnected claims is what Kane (2013) refers to as an interpretation/use argument for the test scores. The interpretation/use argument serves "as the framework for collecting and presenting evidence" for the test score interpretation and use (Kane, 1992, p. 527). In the second stage, the tester uses the interpretation/ use argument for guidance to plan and carry out the research required to seek backing for the assumptions. The four previous chapters illustrated the range of assumptions and suggested some types of investigations that may need to be undertaken. In the third stage, the tester interprets the research and appraises its adequacy for supporting the validity argument. These activities are typically undertaken in a more cyclical, iterative process than the linear progression suggested by the three stages. Nevertheless, the three stages are useful for defining the types of activities that make up the validation process. The following description uses them to outline the process for two scenarios, one for testers working with an existing test and the other for testers designing a new test.

The Interpretation/Use Argument

The first scenario captures a range of situations in which a test has been developed in the past and is currently in use. Tests in use affect the lives of test takers and therefore require continuing attention, including revision, from testers responsible for them. The number and type of testers providing such attention, however, varies dramatically from one test to another, but some of the roles testers might play include those listed in the top-left cell of Table 7.1. For an existing test, the interpretation/use argument needs to be formulated by critically reexamining the past validation research and experience. Testers may have access to years of operational data and research reports, but typically such data have not been interpreted and organized to serve in an explicit validity argument. Experience with test development, use, and marketing should also serve in building an understanding of what the test is intended to accomplish and for whom. Established tests also attract the attention of other users, competitors, and researchers who act as external evaluators providing critical views relevant to developing the interpretation/use argument. All of these perspectives can be brought to bear on the analysis questions provided in Figure 7.3, which are intended to guide testers through the process of conceptualizing an interpretation/use argument by considering the types of claims that they want to make about the test scores.

Column A in Figure 7.3 contains the questions testers can use as a starting point to identify the claims implicit in the current test interpretation and use. The questions, which can be answered initially with a "yes" or "no," refer to the concepts presented throughout the book. Depending on the response to each question in column A, the tester can proceed on the path indicating either "no" to not include a particular type of claim in the validity argument or "yes" to conduct a further analysis of the area. The next steps of the analysis appear in Columns C through E. The questions in Column C ask the tester to identify the existing documentation that pertains to any issue identified by the tester as important for test score interpretation

Figure 7.3 Guidance for Planning an Interpretation/Use Argument for an Existing Test

A. Analysis Questions	B. Contingent Action	C. Backing	D. Warrants and Assumptions	E. Target Research
1. Was a domain analyzed to create tasks that are relevant to the intended test interpretation and use?	If no, no domain definition claim and inference. / If yes, what is the domain?	What evidence do you have that the domain was analyzed appropriately?	See Chapter 6 →	Evaluate existing evidence and plan to gather more.
2. Do the test administration and scoring of performance affect the test scores?	If no, no evaluation claim and inference. / If yes, what are the factors that influence the scores?	What evidence do you have that these factors have not inappropriately influenced scores?	See Chapter 5 →	Evaluate existing evidence and plan to gather more.
3. Are the test scores intended to reflect performance consistency?	If no, no generalization claim and inference / If yes, what are potential sources if inconsistency reflected in the scores?	What estimates do you have about the magnitude of inconsistency for each source?	See Chapter 5 →	Evaluate existing evidence and plan to gather more.
4. Has a construct been defined to serve as a basis for the score interpretation?	If no, no explanation claim and inference / If yes, what is the name of your construct and what type of construct is it?	What evidence do you have about the construct the test measures?	See Chapter 4 →	Evaluate existing evidence and plan to gather more.
5. Have you defined the domain for which your scores are relevant?	If no, no extrapolation claim and inference / If yes, what is the target domain?	What evidence do you have about how well scores reflect the performance in the target domain?	See Chapter 4 →	Evaluate existing evidence and plan to gather more.
6. Do you have a use for your test scores?	If no, no utilization claim and inference / If yes, what decisions or actions are taken based on test results?	What evidence do you have about the utility of test scores for these uses?	See Chapter 3 →	Evaluate existing evidence and plan to gather more.
7. Have you identified the intended effects or implications of your test scores?	If no, no utilization claim and inference / If yes, what are the intended consequences of the test scores?	What evidence do you have about the consequences of test the scores?	See Chapter 3 →	Evaluate existing evidence and plan to gather more.

and use. In other words, the questions in Column C prompt the tester to track down and assemble existing research and practices that play a role in developing the validity argument. Column D identifies the chapter relevant for formulating the respective warrants and assumptions. Chapters 3 through 6 define the types of warrants that can be used to support each inference and examples of assumptions.

The tester should determine whether or not each type of warrant is relevant for support of the inference leading to the particular claim. If a type of warrant is appropriate, the examples in the respective chapters can be used for writing the specific warrants relevant to the test. For these warrants to be included in the validity argument, the assumptions should be written by taking into account three considerations: The examples of assumptions provided in the previous chapters, the results from the existing research and practice, and the specific support logically required for a particular assumption in the context. Professionals may vary in their views of what assumptions should be stated for warrants in a particular case, so these need to be agreed upon and stated by those responsible for the test. Column E directs testers to evaluate existing research and to target additional research required for support of assumptions. The amount of evidence required for support of each assumption depends on factors such as the nature of the assumption, who needs to be convinced of its credibility, and its importance in the validity argument.

The second scenario depicts the situations where the validity argument is being developed for a new test or a test is being substantially revised for use in a new situation. In this case, the testers formulate an interpretation/ use argument as part of their test development activities. The new test is intended to respond to a mandate which may or may not be specified precisely. The analysis questions in Column A of Figure 7.4 help the tester to understand the mandate in greater detail by identifying the types of claims to be made on the basis of the test scores. Each of the questions can be answered initially with a "yes" or "no," and the appropriate action of making a particular claim or not making the claim should then be taken. If the response is "yes," the follow-up question in Column B can be used to prompt the additional specification required for formulating a claim. Column C directs testers to the respective chapter for considering how to express the claims, identify the relevant inferences, and compose the supporting warrants and assumptions. Column D asks the tester to plan the research needed to support each assumption.

The result of these processes is an interpretation/use argument that identifies the research to be undertaken to support a validity argument. In this sense, it provides a test-use specific framework. This first draft of the interpretation/use argument may need to be revised as research is conducted and

113

Figure 7.4 Guidance for Planning an Interpretation/Use Argument for a New Test

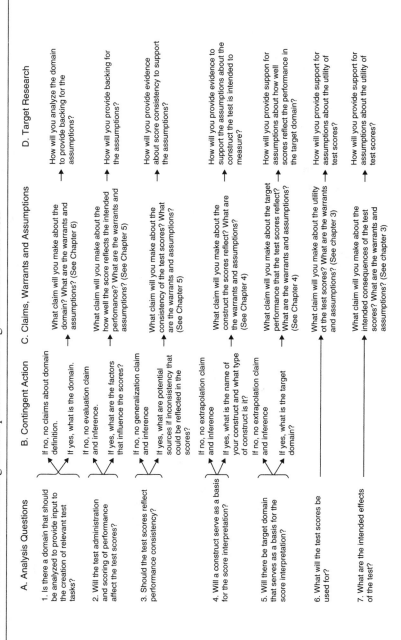

results are interpreted. Nevertheless, it provides an initial framework for grounding validation research in the logic and detail of the specific interpretation/use argument for the test.

Validation Research

As the previous four chapters have shown, validation research needs to address a variety of different types of claims about scores encompassing such meanings as their real world relevance, substantive sense, functional role, and stability. Such diverse meanings require research undertaken using a variety of methodologies including both qualitative and quantitative research as suggested by the five types of evidence indicated in the *Standards*. Table 7.2 provides some examples of the types of qualitative and quantitative methodologies that may be used to investigate assumptions underlying the warrants for each of the inferences. In the previous chapters some references to examples of research were given, but each methodology, whether it be surveys, quantitative modeling, interviews, or introspection, for example, has a substantial research methodological tradition that testers can draw upon. The combination of quantitative and qualitative methods within a single methodological framework, however, falls within the methodological tradition of mixed-methods research.

Mixed-methods researchers present their methods as holding the middle ground between the philosophical and methodological traditions of quantitative and qualitative approaches to research. Johnson and Gray (2010) connect modern mixed-methods researchers to a long history of scholars whose world views and practical needs prompt compromise between the two extremes of positivism and interpretivism that undergird quantitative and qualitative methods, respectively. Today, this middle ground finds a philosophical home in elements of pragmatism (Biesta, 2010).

With respect to methodology, Creswell and Plano-Clark (2018) identified the four characteristics of mixed methods outlined on the left side of Table 7.3. The right side of Table 7.3 presents the corresponding methodological characteristics of validation as mixed-methods research. First, mixed-methods research collects and analyzes both qualitative and quantitative data in response to research questions and hypotheses. Argument-based validation research engages the same combination of data collection and analysis. The interpretation/use argument provides the initial framework for doing so by identifying the warrants that serve as hypotheses in need of testing, and the assumptions that provide motivation for specific research questions.

Table 7.2   Examples of Quantitative and Qualitative Research Methods
Used to Investigate Seven Inferences in a Validity Argument

Inference in a Validity Argument	Example of Quantitative Research Supporting an Assumption	Example of Qualitative Research Supporting an Assumption
Consequence Implication	Survey of teachers' opinions of the value of a mandated achievement test for improving students' learning	Interviews with students about their test preparation practices after a new high-stakes test has been instituted
Utilization	Descriptive statistics of test scores showing acceptable discrimination at proposed cut scores	Classroom observations of students placed into certain classes based on test scores
Extrapolation	Correlation of test scores with scores intended to reflect the target performance	Discourse analysis comparing the linguistic features of test takers' constructed responses with those of their performance on similar tasks in the target domain
Explanation	Structural equation modeling testing the role of theorized components of the construct	Think-aloud retrospective accounts of test-taking processes
Generalization	A G-study investigating the reliability obtained with varying numbers of tasks and raters	Think-aloud study of raters decision-making processes while rating constructed responses across test forms
Evaluation	Item analysis to calculate difficulty, discrimination, and model fit	Observational study of security protocols as they are carried out at test centers
Domain Definition	Survey of content experts about importance of prospective test content	Focus group conducted with content experts to explore the range of content coverage desired for a test

Table 7.3   Core Characteristics of Mixed-Methods Research and the
Corresponding Practices in Argument-Based Validity

Core Characteristics of Mixed-Methods Research	Validation as Mixed-Methods Research
Collects and analyzes both qualitative and quantitative data rigorously in response to research questions and hypotheses	Collects and analyzes both qualitative and quantitative data to address research questions motivated by assumptions and hypotheses set up by warrants
Integrates (or mixes or combines) the two forms of data and their results	Integrates the two forms of data and their results to arrive at a judgment about the validity of test interpretation and use
Organizes these procedures into specific research designs that provide the logic and procedures for conducting the study	Uses the interpretation/use argument to organize these procedures according to the logic of the argument
Frames these procedures within theory and philosophy (Creswell & Plano-Clark, 2018, p. 5)	Frames these procedures within validation theory and typically pragmatist philosophy of science

Second, mixed-methods research integrates the two forms of data in ways that have been explicated and accepted in social science research, in part because of the appearance of methodology textbooks and handbooks, journals and articles, as well as widespread use (e.g., Tashakkori, & Teddlie, 2010). The establishment of mixed methods over the past 30 years probably exceeds what Cronbach could have presaged when he wrote in 1971, "Validation of an instrument calls for an integration of many types of evidence. The varieties of investigation are not alternatives any one of which would be adequate. The investigations supplement one another" (p. 445). Like Messick and Kane after him, Cronbach saw the various forms of research used in validation as pieces of a whole. "For purposes of exposition, it is necessary to subdivide *what in the end must be a comprehensive, integrated evaluation of the test*" (p. 445). In this sense, the tester's challenge in interpretation is that of the mixed-methods researcher. The challenge differs only in the clarity of the overall questions that must be addressed, which are specified for the tester in the interpretation/use argument.

Third, the mixed-methods researcher organizes qualitative and quantitative procedures into specific research designs that provide the logic and procedures for conducting the study. Research methodology textbooks such as the one by Creswell and Plano-Clark (2018) supply the logic, vocabulary and notation for expressing various elements of design (e.g., sequential, explanatory, embedded). Use of these design elements can transform a basket full of procedures into a design with order and purpose that provides clarity for the researchers and a means of communicating to others about its substance and logic. Argument-based validity research provides the interpretation/use argument as an overall framework for organizing the variety of research procedures according to the logic of the argument. The examples in this book hint at some variations in overall logic that can be expressed through the inclusion or omission of particular inferences (e.g., see Chapter 4). However, the range of warrants and assumptions used to support inferences in various contexts can create variations in designs that have yet to be explored. Whereas mixed-methods methodology has become better understood with its use in many studies and ongoing discussion about methodology, argument-based validity has not yet benefited from such broad engagement in its discourse community. Like debate about research methodology in the past, academic discussion about validity and validation to date has tended to be either philosophical or technical, leaving the middle ground of methodology much less attended to.

Fourth, mixed-methods research frames the procedures and logic of the research within its theoretically based motivation and philosophy. With respect to validity argument, for example, some testers wish to treat construct theory as true, which they can do by stating their claims, warrants, and assumptions for explanation accordingly. Rather than assuming a single, uniform theoretical conception underlying all validity arguments, mixed-methods researchers are responsible for making explicit the theoretical basis for their validation research. Messick's (1989) chapter explicated validity inquiry though multiple philosophical lenses. He also outlined the implications of different theoretical perspectives for construct meaning as a sign (trait), sample (performance), or a combination of the two (interactionalist). Despite the fundamental importance of these issues for understanding what validation is, the philosophical threads of Messick's chapter have been barely followed. An exception appeared in a book titled *Frontiers of Test Validity Theory* by Markus and Borsboom (2014), which provides a substantial inquiry into the philosophical basis of validation of tests and assessments. The ideal for mixed-methods research—not yet realized in validation research—is that the tester-researcher would be able to articulate the perspectives taken in a validity argument with respect to their philosophical bases. The book by Markus and Borsboom and the discussion of philosophical bases for mixed-methods research (e.g., Biesta, 2010) together provide a starting point for testers wishing to pursue this goal.

The Validity Argument

Research results that pertain to assumptions in the interpretation/use argument are used to develop the validity argument. The validity argument includes the claims, inferences, warrants, and assumptions that are supported by statements about practice and research findings. Complete backing should exist as records of test development and quality control procedures as well as reports of research. This type of documentation is needed for clarity of procedures internally, for allowing replication research to be undertaken, and for review of the validity argument externally. It is the responsibility of testers who manage testing programs to see that the validation research is summarized and interpreted in a manner that results in a validity argument supporting the claims that the testing program makes about interpretations and uses of the test.

Validity arguments ideally have their origins with internal team members, but they need to communicate beyond the team. A testing program needs to communicate across discourse communities, shown in Figure 7.2, as well as to the public. Figure 7.2 shows professional communities of the field-specific testing community as well as the more general community of researchers in educational and psychological testing. The former may or may not have a well-developed community in which certain norms exist for reporting on validation practices. Whether or not field-specific norms have been developed, testing in all fields is largely under the jurisdiction of the norms of educational and psychological testing, as reflected in the *Standards*. Within this jurisdiction, professionals need to have a consistent understanding of the validity argument genre to guide their practice and communication, in part to serve as external evaluators for each other.

A shared understanding among professionals is the driving force behind the consensus definition of validity that appears in the *Standards*. Shepard (2016) recognized that such coherence within the field is also critical for communication beyond the discourse communities of professionals. With respect to the definition of validity, solidarity is critical because the field has

started with a common word and built its specialised meanings on top of it. The vocabulary of social science is embedded in institutional and legal contexts and laden with associated connotations. Unlike the vocabulary of the natural sciences, "validity" is a term used in the context of evaluating teachers and students and controlling access to higher education, employment, gifted education and so forth. It would be an inappropriate bait-and-switch tactic to deploy a narrower definition in these contexts in which validity is the more complex and decision-directed idea developed in the broader institutional–legal context. (p. 271)

When the term *validity* is used by professionals, the definition should carry with it the genre knowledge of how validation is carried out. In other words, like the term *validity,* the genre of validity argument is intended to serve as an instrument of solidarity within the field, which in turn supports communication beyond the field and education of test users across many different applied areas, where the *Standards* is treated as authoritative (e.g., Lenz & Wester, 2017). In the interest of clarifying and building upon the professional knowledge, this book has elaborated on the consensus definition of validity in the *Standards* by presenting argument-based validation as a professional genre for doing validation.

This book stopped short of exploring ways of transforming the professional genre to the many audiences in the public who may take an interest in how researchers arrive at claims about validity. Testers communicating with people outside the field need to recognize that for the public, validity can have any number of positive meanings, such as "good," "credible," "trustworthy," and "fair," for a particular context. However, the public expects professional testers to be able to elaborate how they know when they see validity and to communicate with other testers using a common professional language. One of the functions of argument-based validity is to serve as a basis for creating audience-appropriate validity narratives, some that communicate with other professionals, including external evaluators, and others that elaborate the basis for validity claims across audiences. One critically important audience is the practitioners who need the skills to appraise an ever-growing selection of assessments for every applied area.

Conclusion

This chapter placed argument-based validity in its sociocultural context, where it serves as a genre for doing and communicating about validation within professional communities. It depicted such professional communities of educational and psychological testing situated within the larger public, with whom professionals communicate using different language. The need to communicate with the public was the primary impetus for Cronbach's invitation for the profession to think of validity argument, rather than validation research, and for Kane to formulate how to do so. This book takes the next step by consolidating the knowledge of argument-based validity as a genre, with the aim of improving consistency and expanding its use by professionals so that they are equipped to use the genre and participate in its future evolution. These goals of improving communication within the profession are fundamental to improved communication with the public.

120

The book does not attempt to transform argument-based validity for nonspecialists. Instead, argument-based validity serves as the basis from which testers communicate interpretations of technical work within an audience-appropriate narrative. As members of the public, testers are capable of choosing their language judiciously to communicate the same basic message to different people, from their first-year graduate students to their colleagues in the field and a neighbor who works in wealth management, marketing, or automobile maintenance. People succeed in communicating with diverse audiences by taking into account what they know and are interested in and by tailoring communication accordingly.

The need to communicate about validity, of course, assumes a society in which the public has an interest because it has a voice, test users have choices, and test developers have professional responsibilities. In other words, the genre of argument-based validity grew to serve a social function in a society where evidence-based arguments are a valued as a means of understanding and decision making. Because the field of educational and psychological assessment transcends borders, Figure 7.2 could include at least one additional circle outside of the public, which would represent the sociocultural values and norms for testing and would include governments and their role in decision making. It remains to be seen whether and how argument-based validity is repurposed to serve in societies where decisions about testing are handled differently.

REFERENCES

Allen, J. L., Sylask, K. M., & Mayer, J. (2016). Emotional intelligence. In V. Zeigler-Hill & T. K. Shackelford (Eds.), *Encyclopedia of personality and individual differences* (pp. 1–6). New York: Springer.

American Education Research Association, American Psychological Association, & the National Council on Measurement in Education. (2014). *Standards for educational and psychological testing.* Washington, DC: American Education Research Association.

Bachman, L. F., & Palmer, A. S. (2010). *Language assessment in practice.* Oxford, UK: Oxford University Press.

Bennett, R. E., & Bajar, I. I. (1998). Validity and automated scoring: It's not only the scoring. *Educational Measurement: Issues and Practice, 17,* 9–17.

Biber, D., Conrad, S. M., Reppen, R., Byrd, P., Helt, M., Clark, V., Cortez, V., Csomay, E., & Urzua, A. (2004). *Representing language use in the university: Analysis of the TOEFL 2000 spoken and written academic language corpus* (TOEFL Monograph Series No. 25). Princeton, NJ: Educational Testing Service.

Biesta, G. (2010). Pragmatism and the philosophical foundations of mixed methods research. In A. Tashakkori & C. Teddlie, (Eds.), *SAGE handbook of mixed methods in social & behavioral research* (2nd ed., pp. 95–117). Thousand Oaks, CA: SAGE.

Borsboom, D. (2006). The attack of the psychometricians. *Psychometrika, 71,* 425–440.

Brackett, M. A., & Mayer, J. D. (2003). Convergent, discriminant, and incremental validity of competing measures of emotional intelligence. *Personality and Social Psychology Bulletin, 29,* 1147–1158.

Brennan, R. L. (1983). *Elements of generalizability theory.* Iowa City, IA: American College Testing Program.

Brennan, R. L. (1998). Misconceptions at the intersection of measurement theory and practice. *Educational Measurement: Issues and Practice, 17*(1), 5–9, 30.

Brennan, R. L. (2001). An essay on the history and future of reliability from the perspective of replications. *Journal of Educational Measurement, 38*(4), 295–317.

Brennan, R. (2013). Commentary on "Validating the interpretations and uses of test scores." *Journal of Educational Measurement, 50*(1), 74–83.

Bridgeman, B., Cho, Y., & DiPietro, S. (2016). Predicting grades from an English-language assessment: The importance of peeling the onion. *Language Testing, 33*(3), 307–318.

Brooks, L., & Swain, M. (2014). Contextualizing performances: Comparing performances during TOEFL iBT™ and real-life academic speaking activities. *Language Assessment Quarterly, 11*(4), 353–373.

Camilli, G. (2006). Test fairness. In R. Brennan (Ed.), *Educational measurement* (4th ed., pp. 221–256). Westport, CT: Greenwood.

Campbell, D. T., & Fiske, D. W. (1959). Convergent and discriminant validation by the multitrait-multimethod matrix. *Psychological Bulletin, 56*(2), 81–105.

Chapelle, C. A., Enright, M. E., & Jamieson, J. (Eds.) (2008). *Building a validity argument for the Test of English as a Foreign Language.* London: Routledge.

Chapelle, C. A., Enright, M. E., & Jamieson, J. (2010). Does an argument-based approach to validity make a difference? *Educational Measurement: Issues and Practice, 29*(1), 3–13.

Chapelle, C. A., Schmidgall, J., Lopez, A., Blood, I., Wain, J., Cho, Y., Hutchison, A., Lee, H-W., & Dursun, A. (2018). *Designing a prototype tablet-based learning-oriented assessment for middle school English learners: An evidence-centered design approach* (ETS Research Report). Princeton, NJ: Educational Testing Service.

Cho, Y., & Bridgeman, B. (2012). Relationship of TOEFL iBT scores to academic performance: Some evidence from American universities. *Language Testing, 29*(3), 421–442.

Cizek, G. J. (2012). Defining and distinguishing validity: Interpretations of score meaning and justification of test use. *Psychological Methods, 17*(1), 31–43.

Clauser, B. E., Kane, M. T., & Swanson, D. B. (2002). Validity issues for performance-based tests scored with computer-automated scoring systems. *Applied Measurement in Education, 15*(4), 413–432.

Creswell, J., & Plano Clark, V. (2017). *Designing and conducting mixed methods research* (3rd ed.). Thousand Oaks, CA: SAGE.

Crocker, L. (1997). The great validity debate. *Educational Measurement: Issues and Practice, 16*(2), 4.

Cronbach, L. J. (1951). Coefficient alpha and the internal structure of tests. *Psychometrika, 16,* 297–334.

Cronbach, L. J. (1971). Test validation. In R. Thorndike (Ed.), *Educational measurement* (2nd ed., pp. 443–507). Washington, DC: American Council on Education.

Cronbach, L. (1988). Five perspectives on validity argument. In H. Wainer & H. Braun (Eds.), *Test validity* (pp. 3–17). Hillsdale, NJ: Lawrence Erlbaum.

Cronbach, L. J., & Meehl, P. E. (1955). Construct validity in psychological tests. *Psychological Bulletin, 52,* 281–302.

Cureton, E. E. (1951). Validity. In E. F. Lindquist (Ed.), *Educational measurement* (pp. 621–694). Washington, DC: American Council on Education.

DiBello, L. V., Pellegrino, J. W., Gane, B. D., & Goldman, S. R. (2017). The contribution of student response processes to validity analyses for instructionally supportive assessments. In K. W. Ercikan & J. W. Pellegrino (Eds.), *Validation of score meaning in the next generation of assessments: The use of response processes* (pp. 85–99). New York: Routledge.

Educational Testing Service. (2002). *ETS standards for quality and fairness.* Princeton, NJ: Author.

Educational Testing Service. (2005). *Standard-setting materials for the Internet-based TOEFL test* [Compact disc]. Princeton, NJ: Author.

Educational Testing Service. (2010). *TOEFL iBT™ test framework and test development* (TOEFL iBT™ Research Insight, Vol. 1, Series 1). Princeton, NJ: Author.

Educational Testing Service (2011a). *Supporting the interpretation and use of TOEFL IBT™ scores* (TOEFL iBT™ Research Insight, Vol. 1, Series 4). Princeton, NJ: Author.

Educational Testing Service. (2011b). *Reliability and comparability of TOEFL iBT™ scores* (TOEFL iBT™ Insight, Vol. 1, Series 3). Princeton, NJ: Author.

Educational Testing Service. (2012). *TOEFL iBT^{TM} test prep planner.* Princeton, NJ: Author.

Embretson, S. E. (1983). Construct validity: Construct representation versus nomothetic span. *Psychological Bulletin, 93*(1), 179–197.

Ercikan, K. W., & Pellegrino, J. W. (Eds.). (2017). *Validation of score meaning in the next generation of assessments. The use of response processes.* New York, NY: Routledge.

Feldt, L. S., & Brennan, R. L. (1989). Reliability. In R. L. Linn (Ed.), *Educational measurement* (3rd ed.; pp. 105–146). New York, NY: Macmillan.

Ginther, A., & Yan, X. (2018). Interpreting the relationships between TOEFL iBT scores and GPA: Language proficiency, policy, and profiles. *Language Testing, 35*(2), 271–295.

Goeman, J. J., & De Jong, N. H. (2018). How well does the sum score summarize the test? Summability as a measure of internal consistency. *Educational Measurement: Issues and Practice, 37*(2), 54–63.

Gould, S. J. (1996). *The mismeasure of man* (rev. and expanded ed.). New York: W. W. Norton & Company.

Gronlund, N. E. (1985). *Measurement and evaluation in teaching* (5th ed.). New York, NY: Macmillan.

Haertel, E. H. (2006). Reliability. In R. L. Brennan (Ed.), *Educational measurement* (4th ed., pp. 65–110). Westport, CT: Praeger.

Haertel, E. (2013). Getting the help we need. *Journal of Educational Measurement, 50*(1), 84–90.

Hambleton, R. K., & Pitoniak, M. J. (2006). Setting performance standards. In R. L. Brennan (Ed.), *Educational measurement* (4th ed., pp. 433–470). Westport, CT: Praeger.

Hambleton, R. K., Swaminathan, H., & Rogers, H. J. (1991). *Fundamentals of item response theory.* Thousand Oaks, CA: SAGE.

Horn, J. L., & Cattell, R. B. (1966). Refinement and test of the theory of fluid and crystallized general intelligences. *Journal of Educational Psychology, 57,* 253–270.

Hubley, A. M., & Zumbo, B. D. (2017). Response processes in the context of validity: Setting the stage. In B. D. Zumbo & A. M. Hubley (Eds.), *Understanding and investigating response processes in validation research* (pp. 1–12). Cham, Switzerland: Springer.

Johnson, B., & Gray, R. (2010). A history of philosophical and theoretical issues for mixed methods research. In A. Tashakkori & C. Teddlie,

(Eds.), *SAGE handbook of mixed methods in social & behavioral research* (2nd ed., pp. 69–94). Thousand Oaks, CA: SAGE.

Kane, M. T. (1992). An argument-based approach to validity. *Psychological Bulletin, 112,* 527–535.

Kane, M. T. (1994). Validating interpretive arguments for licensure and certification examinations. *Evaluation and the Health Professions, 17*(2), 133–159.

Kane, M. T. (2001). Current concerns in validity theory. *Journal of Educational Measurement, 38,* 319–342.

Kane, M. T. (2002). Validating high-stakes testing programs. *Educational Measurement: Issues and Practices, 21*(1), 31–41.

Kane, M. T. (2004). Certification testing as an illustration of argument-based validation. *Measurement, 2*(3), 135–170.

Kane, M. (2006). Validation. In R. Brennan, (Ed.), *Educational measurement* (4th ed., pp. 17–64). Westport, CT: Praeger.

Kane, M. T. (2013). Validating the interpretations and uses of test scores. *Journal of Educational Measurement, 50*(1), 1–73.

Kane, M. T. (2016). Explicating validity, *Assessment in Education: Principles, Policy & Practice, 23*(2), 198–211.

Kane, M., Crooks, T., & Cohen, A. (1999). Validating measures of performance. *Educational Measurement: Issues and Practice, 18*(2), 5–17.

Kane, M., & Mislevy, R. (2017). Validating score interpretations based on response processes. In K. W. Ercikan & J. W. Pellegrino (Eds.), *Validation of score meaning in the next generation of assessments: The use of response processes* (pp. 11–24). New York, NY: Routledge.

Kokhan, K. (2012). Investigating the possibility of using TOEFL scores for university ESL decision-making: Placement trends and effect of time lag. *Language Testing, 29*(2), 291–308.

Kolen, M. J., & Brennan, R. L. (1995). *Test equating: Methods and practices.* New York, NY: Springer-Verlag.

Kuss, D. J., Shorter G. W., van Rooij, A. J., van de Mheen, D., & Griffiths, M. D. (2014). The internet addiction components model and personality: Establishing construct validity via a nomological network. *Computers in Human Behavior, 39,* 312–321.

Lee, Y.-W., & Kantor, R. (2005). *Dependability of new ESL writing test scores: Evaluating prototype tasks and alternative rating schemes* (ETS Research Report RR-05-14). Princeton, NJ: ETS.

Lenz, A. S., & Wester, K. L. (2017). Development and evaluation of assessments for counseling professionals. *Measurement and Evaluation in Counseling and Development, 50,* 201–209.

Lissitz, R. W. (Ed.). (2009). *The concept of validity: Revisions new directions and applications.* Charlotte, NC: Information Age.

Lissitz, R. W., & Samuelsen, K. (2007). Dialogue on validity: A suggested change in terminology and emphasis regarding validity and education. *Educational Researcher, 36,* 437–448.

Llosa, L., & Malone, M. (2018). Comparability of students' writing performance on TOEFL iBT and required university writing courses. *Language Testing, 36*(2), 235–263.

Lord, F. M. (1980). *Applications of item response theory to practical testing problems.* Hillsdale, NJ: Erlbaum.

MacCann, C., Pearce, N., & Roberts, R. D. (2011). Emotional intelligence as assessed by situational judgement and emotion recognition tests: Building the nomological net. *Psychological Topics, 20*(3), 393–412.

Markus, K. A., & Borsboom, D. (2013). *Frontiers of test validity theory: Measurement, causation, and meaning.* New York, NY: Routledge.

Mayer, J. D., Caruso, D. R., & Salovey, P. (2016). The ability model of emotional intelligence: Principles and updates. *Emotion Review, 8*(4), 290–300.

Mayer, J. D., Salovey, P., & Caruso, D. R. (2008). Emotional intelligence: New ability or eclectic traits? *American Psychologist, 63*(6), 503–517.

Mayer, J., Salovey, P., & Caruso, D. R. (2012). The validity of the MSCEIT: Additional analyses and evidence. *Emotion Review, 4*(4), 403–408.

Mayer, J. D., Salovey, P., Caruso, D. R., & Sitarenios, G. (2003). Measuring emotional intelligence with the MSCEIT V2.0. *Emotion, 3*(1), 97–105.

McNamara, T. (1996). *Measuring second language performance.* London, UK: Longman.

Messick, S. (1989). Validity. In R. L. Linn (Ed.), *Educational measurement* (3rd ed., pp. 13–103). New York, NY: Macmillan.

MHS Assessments. (n.d.). *MSCEIT information sheet.* Toronto, ON: Author. Retrieved from http://issuu.com/mhs-assessments/docs/msceit_infosheet? e=20431871/49397409

Mislevy, R. J. (2006). Cognitive psychology and educational measurement. In R. L. Brennan (Ed.), *Educational measurement* (4th ed., pp. 257–305). Westport, CT: Praeger.

Mislevy, R. (2018). *Sociocognitive foundations of educational measurement.* London, UK: Routledge.

Mislevy, R. J., Steinberg, L. S., & Almond, R. G. (2003). On the structure of educational assessments. *Measurement: Interdisciplinary Research and Perspectives, 1*, 3–62.

Moss, P. A. (1994). Can there be validity without reliability? *Educational Researcher, 23*(2), 5–12.

Moss, P. A. (2013). Validity in action: Lessons from studies of data use. *Journal of Educational Measurement, 50*(1), 91–98.

Newton, P. E., & Baird, J.-A. (2016). The great validity debate. *Assessment in Education: Principles, Policy & Practice, 23*(2), 173–177.

Newton, P. E., & Shaw, S. D. (2014). *Validity in educational & psychological assessment.* London, UK: SAGE.

Norris, S. P. (1983). The inconsistencies at the foundation of construct validation theory. In E. R. House (Ed.), *Philosophy of evaluation* (pp. 53–74). San Francisco, CA: Jossey-Bass.

Pearlman, M. (2008). Finalizing the test blueprint. In C. Chapelle, M. K. Enright, & J. M. Jamieson (Eds.), *Building a validity argument for the Test of English as a Foreign Language™,* pp. 227–258. New York, NY: Routledge.

Petersen, N. S., Kolen, M. J., & Hoover, H. D. (1989). Scaling, norming, and equating. In R. L. Linn (Ed.), *Educational measurement* (3rd ed., pp. 221–262). Washington, DC: American Council on Education.

Plake, B. S., & Wise, L. L. (2014). What is the role and importance of the revised AERA, APA, NCME standards for educational and psychological testing? *Educational Measurement: Issues and Practice, 33*(4), 4–12.

Popham, W. J. (1997). Consequential validity: Right concern wrong concept. *Educational Measurement: Issues and Practice, 16*(2), 9–13.

Riazi, A. M. (2016). Comparing writing performance in TOEFL-iBT and academic assignments: An exploration of textual features. *Assessing Writing, 28*, 15–27.

Rosenfeld, M., Leung, P., & Oltman, P. K. (2001). *The reading, writing, speaking, and listening tasks important for academic success at the undergraduate and graduate levels* (TOEFL Monograph No. 21). Princeton, NJ: Educational Testing Services.

Shen, B., Wingert, R. K., Li, W., Sun, H., & Rukavina, P. B. (2010). An amotivation model in physical education. *Journal of Teaching in Physical Education, 29*, 72–84.

Shepard, L. A. (1993). Evaluating test validity. *Review of Research in Education, 19*, 405–450.

Shepard, L. A. (1997). The centrality of test use and consequences for test validity. *Educational Measurement: Issues and Practice, 16*(2), 5–24.

Shepard, L. (2016). Evaluating test validity: Reprise and progress. *Assessment in Education: Principles, Policy & Practice, 23*(2), 268–280.

Sireci, S. G. (1998a). The construct of content validity. *Social Indicators Research, 45,* 83–117.

Sireci, S. G. (1998b). Gathering and analyzing content validity data. *Educational Assessment, 5,* 299–321.

Sireci, S. G. (2009). Packing and unpacking sources of validity evidence: History repeats itself again. In R. Lissitz (Ed.), *The concept of validity: Revisions, new directions and applications* (pp. 19–37). Charlotte, NC: Information Age.

Sireci, S. G. (2013). Agreeing on validity arguments. *Journal of Educational Measurement, 50*(1), 99–104.

Sireci, S. G. (2016). On the validity of useless tests. *Assessment in Education: Principles, Policy & Practice, 23*(2), 226–235.

Sireci, S., & Faulkner-Bond, M. (2014). Validity evidence based on test content. *Psicothema, 26*(1), 100–107.

Slaney, K. (2017). *Validating psychological constructs: Historical, philosophical, and practical dimensions.* London, UK: Palgrave Macmillan.

Swales, J. (1990). *Genre analysis*: English in academic and research settings. Cambridge, UK: Cambridge University Press.

Tashakkori, A., & Teddlie, C. (Eds.). (2010). *SAGE handbook of mixed methods in social & behavioral research* (2nd ed.). Thousand Oaks, CA: SAGE.

Taylor, C., & Angelis, P. (2008). The evolution of the TOEFL. In C. A. Chapelle, M. E. Enright, & J. Jamieson (Eds.), *Building a validity argument for the Test of English as a Foreign Language* (pp. 27–54). London, UK: Routledge.

Toulmin, S. E. (2003). *The uses of argument* (updated ed.). Cambridge, UK: Cambridge University Press.

University of Iowa. (2015). *Research and development guide: Iowa Assessments, Forms E and F.* Iowa City, IA: Author.

Vlachopoulos, S. P., Katartzi, E. S., & Kontou, M. G. (2013). Fitting multidimensional amotivation into the self-determination theory nomological network: Application in school physical education. *Measurement in Physical Education and Exercise Science, 17,* 40–61.

Wall, D., & Horák, T. (2006). *The impact of changes in the TOEFL examination on teaching and learning in central and eastern Europe: Phase 1, the baseline study* (TOEFL Monograph No. MS-34). Princeton, NJ: Educational Testing Service.

Wise, L. L. (2017). Commentary I: Validating score meaning in the next generation of assessments. In K. W. Ercikan & J. W. Pellegrino (Eds.), *Validation of score meaning in the next generation of assessments: The use of response processes* (pp. 52–59). New York, NY: Routledge.

Xi, X. (2008). *Investigating the criterion-related validity of the TOEFL speaking scores for ITA screening and setting standards for ITAs.* (TOEFL iBT Research Report No. TOEFLiBT-03). Princeton, NJ: Educational Testing Service.

Xi, X. (2012). How do we go about investigating test fairness? *Language Testing, 27*(2), 147–170.

Zhang, Y. (2008). *Repeater analyses for TOEFL iBT* (ETS Research Report RM-08-05). Princeton, NJ: ETS.

Zumbo, B. (2014). What role does, and should, the test *Standards* play outside of the United States of America? *Educational Measurement: Issues and Practice, 33*(4), 4-12.

Zwick, R. (2006). Higher education admissions testing. In R. Brennan (Ed.), *Educational Measurement* (4th ed., pp. 221–256). Westport, CT: Greenwood.

INDEX

134